MY DADDY KILLED MY MOMMY

Detective Dylhoff made himself comfortable in the familiar dwelling of Lisa Smith's foster mother. Lisa had recently returned from a weeklong vacation with her real grandparents and father in Ohio. She explained to Dylhoff that while on her trip she slept in the living room so she could avoid being spanked by her father's paddle.

"Are there more things you are afraid of with your daddy than just the paddle?" Dylhoff coaxed.

Lisa nodded, her eyes downcast. "I think my daddy killed my mommy."

"Why do you think that?" Dylhoff asked softly.

"Daddy was very angry at me when I went into the bathroom, when he told me not to. There was also no way that Mommy could kick those big holes in the wall in the bathroom."

From the blood Lisa found in the sink, she believed her father had killed her mother. Lisa struggled not to cry during her conversation with Dylhoff, but she was unab̲l̲e̲ ̲t̲o̲ ̲c̲o̲n̲t̲r̲o̲l̲ ̲t̲h̲e̲ ̲t̲e̲a̲r̲s̲ ̲t̲h̲a̲t̲ ̲f̲e̲l̲l̲ ̲f̲r̲om her eyes.

Other books by Patricia Springer

BLOOD RUSH

MAIL ORDER MURDER

BODY HUNTER

FLESH AND BLOOD

A LOVE TO DIE FOR

BLOOD STAINS

MURDER SO COLD

PATRICIA SPRINGER

PINNACLE BOOKS
Kensington Publishing Corp.
http://www.kensingtonbooks.com

PINNACLE BOOKS are published by

Kensington Publishing Corp.
850 Third Avenue
New York, NY 10022

All Kensington Titles, Imprints, and Distributed Lines are available at special quantity discounts for bulk purchases for sales promotions, premiums, fund-raising, and educational or institutional use. Special book excerpts or customized printings can also be created to fit specific needs. For details, write or phone the office of the Kensington special sales manager: Kensington Publishing Corp., 850 Third Avenue, New York, NY 10022, attn: Special Sales Department, Phone: 1-800-221-2647.

Pinnacle and the P logo Reg. U.S. Pat. & TM Off.

First Pinnacle Printing: January 2004
10 9 8 7 6 5 4

Printed in the United States of America

To Larry Graham,
for all the encouragement and support.

ACKNOWLEDGMENTS

I first met Randy Dylhoff and Mike Werkema on the set of Leeza Gibbons's TV Show. They were there to discuss the murder of Khristine Smith, I to talk about a Texas case. I found both detectives to be charming, passionate about their work, and devoted to their families. Without their candid and insightful accounts of the murder of Khristine Smith, this book would never have been possible. I admire these men and the work they do. And I thank them for their willingness to work with me.

As always, I have to thank my support system, the ones who are always available to help in their areas of expertise to make a project come together. These people are not only my advisers, but also my close friends. Thanks to Tina Church of Specialized Investigative Services, Inc., Jan Blankenship, LPC, Judge Kenny Kirkland, Detective Tom LeNoir, and good friend Edward Lynton.

No project would be complete without the expert scrutiny of LaRee Bryant, editorial consultant. She makes me a better writer through her diligence to my task and a better person for her friendship.

Last, but no means least, I thank Michaela Hamilton of Kensington Publishing for her creative input.

Prologue

September 28, 1994

The headlines of the *Kalamazoo Gazette* were scattered with news of violent men and the women who faced their fury.

O.J. SIMPSON ON TRIAL

Second day of jury selection in O.J. Simpson trial begins.

BOBBITT GUILTY OF ASSAULT, LABELED A BULLY

John Bobbitt convicted of a second domestic battery charge.

MAN ENTERS PLEA IN ASSAULT

A Kalamazoo man who said he loved his estranged wife "too much to let her go" pleaded no contest to assault with intent to commit murder.

Leaving the newspaper open on the breakfast table, Russ Smith walked hand in hand with his seven-year-old daughter to the bus stop in front of their home on

Thunderbay in Portage, Michigan. Lisa's sandy blond hair glistened in the sunlight of the bright September morning. The little girl chattered happily, oblivious to her father's uncharacteristic silence.

Usually Lisa's mother, Khris, was the one who stood by the roadside to make certain she was safely on the bus headed for school. Khris Smith would then dress and leave for her part-time job at KinderCare Day Care Center. But on this morning Lisa's mother was already preparing for work and her father had taken on the task.

Smith's fingers tightened around his daughter's tiny hand as he leaned down to give her a kiss.

"I love you," Smith whispered.

Lisa smiled. "I love you too, Daddy," Lisa said as she stepped on board the bus and waved exuberantly to her father.

Lisa Smith took her seat, unaware that her life was about to change forever.

Part 1

Chapter 1

It was a brisk 40 degrees, with light rain and a northwest wind, when Russ Smith knocked on his neighbor's door.

"I need you to do me a favor," Russ Smith told Tom Huss on the afternoon of September 30, 1994.

"Sure," Huss said, thinking his neighbor had come to borrow a tool or needed help loading something into his pickup truck.

Smith stepped inside the Huss home, leaving his jacket zipped as he talked with his neighbor. He spoke without apparent anxiety or anger.

"Khris moved out Wednesday," Smith said. "She was having an affair and she wanted to be with someone else."

Huss's jaw dropped in surprise. He was familiar with the Smiths, who lived only a few houses down from him on Thunderbay, but they rarely spoke and weren't what Huss would consider close friends.

All he knew about Khris Smith was that she could often be seen in the driveway of her home washing her car in spiked heels and short shorts. The five-foot-five-inch, slim, attractive brunette had been the talk of her neighbors in the well-kept middle class Portage, Michigan, neighborhood.

Portage, a large suburban city in Kalamazoo County,

had been home to the Smiths for nearly two years. The historic city, settled in 1830, had a strong economy and was considered the main shopping area in the Kalamazoo region. Smith, who was manager of the Sears Automotive Center, had done well in his new managerial position. He liked the city and its people. Khris, on the other hand, had appeared restless and discontent.

"I've spoken to Khris's mother, Kay, in Florida. She told me Khris was having an affair and it's been going on for about three months," Smith continued.

Huss didn't know how to respond to such intimate details from his neighbor. He just stood and listened.

"Will you keep an eye on the house and contact me if Khris comes back home?" Smith asked.

Since Huss was a fireman who worked a varied on-and-off schedule, the request seemed reasonable. He agreed and Smith wrote out the phone numbers of his parents, his pager, and his own home number.

"What about Lisa?" Huss asked, wondering if Khris had taken the seven-year-old child with her or left her daughter as abruptly as she had apparently left her husband.

"Lisa hasn't asked anything about what's going on. I took her out of school on Wednesday. She's at my parents' house near Lima, Ohio," Smith replied. In reality, Lisa Smith had asked dozens of questions of her father, who had been candid and insensitive when he told his daughter that her mother had left them for another man. "Khris left a note saying she was going to go to Florida. I dropped Lisa off and then headed for Florida. I kept calling [the house], hoping she had changed her mind and had come home."

Still stunned, Huss remained silent. The three Smiths had appeared inseparable to him. He had seen them readying their large boat, the type locals called a "Lake Michigan–going vessel," on the back of Smith's truck to set out for a day of family fun. Smith was a tall, medium-built man, with brown hair and a neatly trimmed mustache; Lisa, a cute sandy-blonde with long curls and an infectious smile; Khris, a sexy but seemingly devoted wife and mother. They had appeared to be an ideal family. Again Huss thought Khris Smith's desertion of both Russ and Lisa extremely odd.

Smith interrupted Huss's thoughts. "Khris finally picked up the [home] phone, but she didn't say anything," Smith stated. "That's when I turned around and headed back to Portage. When I got here, I found Khris's house keys, door opener, and her wedding ring in the house."

Smith's words were delivered in a calm monotone, which made Huss uneasy. How could a man be so passionless about such a hurtful event in his life?

"She'd just cut that ring off and laid it on the kitchen counter. That's where I found it," Smith said dryly.

Huss again wondered how Smith could keep his emotions in check during such a stressful event.

Huss was amazed at Smith's story about his wife, but he was even more astonished when Smith casually pulled photos from his pocket and began detailing a recent fishing trip. Huss was unaware that Smith enjoyed fishing. Smith appeared to be more of a ski enthusiast.

"I'm going back to Ohio and pick up Lisa, then head to Florida. Thanks for keeping an eye out for Khris. Call me if you see her," Smith said before leaving the Huss house. Huss watched as Smith returned to his own residence, only a few doors down from the Huss home.

A short time later, Huss watched with curiosity as his neighbor put the garbage bin out by the curb for a Monday pickup, then drove away with Lisa's rabbit in the back of his pickup truck. The bed of the truck also held a black fifty-five-gallon drum.

How strange, Huss thought as he noticed Khristine's 1989 brown Plymouth Sundance parked in the street in front of the house. *Why would she leave her car?*

Huss had more questions than answers when he later spoke to his wife, Kathy, about Khris Smith's sudden exodus. Like her husband, Kathy thought it weird that Khris would just leave Lisa and Russ so suddenly. When he couldn't shake a number of disturbing possibilities, Tom Huss phoned the Portage Police Department to report a suspicious situation. Khris Smith's disappearance might be nothing more than the result of a marital squabble, but Tom thought Russ Smith's story about Khris walking away from her family was too bizarre to be believed. Tom Huss didn't know what was going on; he only had a gut feeling that something was terribly wrong.

When the call came into the Portage Police Department concerning a missing person named Khris Smith on Thunderbay, Detective Randy Dylhoff volunteered to take a look into it.

"Looks like a typical spouse thing," Dylhoff told his supervisor. "A couple of weeks, she'll be back, and I can close it out."

The detective drove to the address given for the Smiths and approached the home of Tim and Debbie Orosz next door.

Dylhoff was merely making a preliminary inquiry based on the Huss report, not a formal investigation. His call on the Smiths' neighbors was more of a fact-finding mission to discover the whereabouts of Khris Smith.

Dylhoff, well over six feet five inches, and well built, towered over the short, stocky couple as he asked about the Oroszes' neighbors.

"Khris and I became quite close. She came over to the house often," Debbie stated. Debbie had a pleasant smile and appeared more than willing to help with the probe.

"Lisa was everything to Khris," Tim Orosz interjected. "They were inseparable. It would be strange for her to just up and leave without taking Lisa with her."

Debbie seemed anxious to give Dylhoff all the information she had on the Smiths' relationship. She claimed that on numerous occasions Khris had come to the Orosz house wearing dark glasses, which she would leave on the entire time she visited at their home.

"I never asked what was wrong," Debbie Orosz said, but her unspoken implication was that Khris Smith, like nearly 4 million other women in the United States each year, may have been a victim of domestic violence. Six-foot-one-inch Russ Smith was significantly larger than his five-foot-five-inch wife. He outweighed her by some fifty pounds. Debbie Orosz obviously thought Smith capable of battering his wife.

"One time Khris mentioned that she was hungry. I asked her why she hadn't eaten and she said Russ wouldn't let her," Debbie stated, adding to the impression that Russ Smith may have been abusive.

Debbie went on to tell the detective that Russ appeared very demanding and that everything at the Smith house had to be in place when he arrived home.

"Khris did all the yard work and kept the house very neat and clean. She told me dinner had to be on the table at a precise time. Khris would often leave in the middle of things to go home to make sure dinner was done," Debbie said. "She also told me that she had to have sex with Russ on Friday nights, no matter if she wanted it or not."

Dylhoff made notes in his flip book as Debbie Orosz made comment after comment about the lifestyle her friend had apparently been living. He was beginning to get a clearer picture of the kind of woman Khris Smith was, as well as what Russ Smith was like as a husband.

After leaving the Orosz residence and returning to his car, Dylhoff reviewed his notes. Both Tom Huss and the Oroszes advised that, during the approximately eighteen months the Smiths had lived on Thunderbay, at no time had they actually seen Russ Smith assault his wife, nor had they seen any visible marks on her. They agreed that the Smiths kept mostly to themselves and that Russ Smith worked very long hours. Dylhoff stroked his bushy brown mustache that curved downward past his lower lip as he paid particular attention to his notes concerning statements from both Tom Huss and Tim Orosz that Smith had been very open about the number of guns he kept in his house.

Both families had expressed an eerie feeling that something was wrong, continuing to insist that it was unlike Khris to leave so abruptly. There had been no direct mention of problems in the marriage. And, most telling of all, their major concern was that Lisa had been left in her father's care when Khris and Lisa were so very close.

Aware that a domestic homicide occurred every eight days in Michigan, and unable to verify the whereabouts of Khris Smith, Dylhoff decided it was time to contact his sergeant.

Dylhoff waited at the front of the Smiths' two-story home until Sergeant Walt Debruyn arrived. The frame house was pale pink, neatly trimmed in white. A porch swing sat at the right of the door and a blooming flower basket hung to the left. Red blossoms had burst open in the flower beds surrounding the small front porch, their bright color accented by a low white-slatted fence. The property was neat and well maintained. If Debbie Orosz was right and Khris Smith did all the work in maintaining the Smith home, she was to be commended for a job well done.

There was no response when the two officers alternately knocked and rang the front doorbell. Dylhoff noted that the porch lights were on, the garbage bin was out by the curb, and Khris Smith's car was still parked in front of the house, just as Tom Huss had described. There was no light coming from either of the two windows bracketing the double front doors.

Dylhoff and Debruyn checked to see if the doors were locked and the windows latched. They peered through glass not obstructed by curtains on the first floor to see if there were any signs of a disturbance. Finding none, Dylhoff contacted the Portage Fire Department, requesting a hook and ladder truck.

Within minutes firemen were peering through the second-story windows of the Smith home from ladders extended from their familiar red-and-white truck. They found it in the same pristine order that Dylhoff and Debruyn had found the downstairs. Every room in the residence that had not been shielded by curtains or which didn't contain exterior windows was checked.

From all that was visible, the Smith house seemed to be as clean and neat as Debbie Orosz had described.

Russ Smith had transferred to the Portage, Michigan, Sears Automotive Center from Fort Wayne. Portage, a smaller city of about fifty thousand compared to Fort Wayne's population of 205,000, offered the Smiths a small-town atmosphere with big-city resources.

Detective Dylhoff arrived at the Sears store two days after speaking to the Huss and Orosz families. He needed to talk to Russ Smith directly about his wife's reported sudden departure. Before arriving at the store, the detective had already established that Khris Smith was not at the YMCA Domestic Assault Shelter, nor had she ever been a resident of the protective haven.

Dylhoff's hopes of speaking to Smith were thwarted. Smith was on vacation and he still had an additional week of leave remaining. Employees at Sears were unable to give Dylhoff a precise date when Smith was expected to return.

Dylhoff was disappointed. If Smith knew where Khris was, the detective could write his report, clear the case, and move on to other open files on his desk. If not, Khris Smith's disappearance more than likely would be upgraded from a suspicious situation to a missing person.

Two days after he was first assigned Khris Smith's case, Dylhoff finally reached Russ Smith on the evening of October 1, at his parents' Ohio home.

"Do you know where Khristine is?" Dylhoff asked.

"No," Smith answered calmly. "I have no idea where she is. She moved out Wednesday and left a note that she wanted to be with someone else. She said she was on her way to Florida."

Smith related the same story to Dylhoff that he'd told

Tom Huss and the Oroszes a few days after she disappeared. Khris was having an affair that had supposedly been going on for about three months. Smith claimed he had learned about his wife's adultery from her mother. He denied that he and Khris had been having any problems. He also denied knowing the identity of the man Khris had been seeing. However, Smith confided in Dylhoff, his wife had had an extramarital liaison approximately two years earlier that had caused a number of problems within their marriage. Smith named Leonard Lavanway as his wife's former lover.

"After I got Khris's note on Wednesday, I took Lisa out of school and took her to my parents' house. Then I headed for Florida to see if I could find Khris," Smith explained.

Once again Smith stated he was near Lexington, Kentucky, when he called home and someone picked up the phone. He claimed he turned back and returned home only to find Khris's keys, garage-door opener, and her wedding ring, which had been cut off, inside the house.

She cut off her wedding ring? Dylhoff thought. It was the second time the detective had heard the unusual reference to the missing woman's wedding band. A woman cutting off her ring was most unusual, as well as being a difficult task without help from someone else. Perhaps her unknown lover had assisted, Dylhoff speculated.

"Can you think of anyone else who was close to Khris that might know where she is?" Dylhoff asked.

"Khris has been working at KinderCare in Portage. She also has a friend by the name of Charlene Lemons," Smith answered. His tone remained controlled.

"Is Lisa with you?" Dylhoff asked.

"Yes," Smith replied. "If you make contact with Khris, have her call me in Ohio. I'd like to talk to her."

After advising Smith to call if he heard anything from Khris, Dylhoff hung up the phone. He paused a few minutes to think about Smith, his relationship with his wife, and the effects of her disappearance on their child. He wondered if the seven-year-old would be able to shed any light on the sudden, unexpected departure of her mother. Dylhoff decided to talk to Lisa as soon as she returned to Michigan with her father.

Charlene Lemons had made friends with Khristine Smith soon after Khris had begun working at the KinderCare Day Care Center. Khris had taken the job as a part-time childcare provider only during the hours Lisa was in school. She hadn't wanted anything to interfere with her ability to be at home with Lisa, to be able to take her to piano and dance lessons, but Khris had wanted her own money—money she didn't have to account for to Russ; money she could save if she ever needed instant funds.

Charlene Lemons told Dylhoff she hadn't seen Khris since September 25, when she had dropped some items off at her house.

"Did Khris ever mention that her marriage was in trouble or that she was having an affair?" Dylhoff asked. The laughter of young children could be heard in the background.

"No, she never mentioned any type of affair or being dissatisfied in her marriage," Lemons answered, apparently caught by surprise by the detective's question.

In response to Dylhoff's inquiry about possible

abuse, Lemons stated she had never seen any marks on Khris that would indicate any type of ill-treatment.

"Khris seemed to be very happy," Lemons told him. "She and Lisa were very close. It seems kind of strange for her to leave and not take Lisa with her."

Dylhoff thought about Lemons's last statement. It was a sentiment expressed by almost everyone he had spoken with. If the reaction of her friends was correct, and Khris Smith wouldn't leave Lisa behind, where was she? And had she moved out of her own free will, as her husband described, or had she left under duress?

Most of Dylhoff's day had been spent on the phone with friends and relatives of the missing woman. He had a couple more calls to make before heading back to the Smith house for another look.

The first call was to Leonard Lavanway, known to his friends as "Lyn," and the man with whom Smith had accused his wife of having a previous affair. Lavanway was taken aback to hear from the police concerning the disappearance of Khris Smith. Lavanway had become friends with Khris when his daughter and Lisa were in the same dance class. Khris had even taken Lisa to the Lavanway residence so the girls could play. He assured Dylhoff that he and Khris were mere acquaintances, although he admitted that Russ Smith had thought something was going on between them at the time.

"Russ called me and threatened to kill me," Lavanway stated. The incident had rattled Lavanway to the point that he had filed a report with the Portage Police Department. "I haven't seen or heard from Khris for nearly two years," Lavanway stated.

Dylhoff leaned back in his chair and stared out his office window at the lush green landscape of the Portage

City Complex. Small evergreens strategically planted on the grassy berms added a sense of serenity.

Was Russ Smith capable of killing? Dylhoff asked himself. Smith displayed no signs of anxiety or guilt. Could he have killed his wife and disposed of her body without so much as a thread of regret or remorse? Russ Smith had to be considered a suspect in the event that Khris Smith was not located, or if evidence of foul play was uncovered. His story didn't correspond with the known behavior of his wife. Dylhoff picked up the phone to make one last call before heading back to the Smiths' home on Thunderbay.

Dylhoff talked briefly with an employee of Kinder-Care in Portage, who verified that Khristine Smith worked a couple of hours a day during lunchtime.

"She didn't show up for work last week on Tuesday, Wednesday, or Thursday. I don't know about Friday," the woman stated.

Dylhoff was told to call back on Monday to find out for certain if Khris Smith had come in on Friday for her scheduled shift at the day care.

Dylhoff slipped into the sport coat that had been hanging on the back of his office chair. Leaving stacks of reports, crime scene photos, and hand-scribbled notes scattered across his desk, he headed toward the Smith house with more questions than answers muddling his mind.

The Smiths' city garbage bin sat at the curb in front of their home, just as it had when Dylhoff and his sergeant first visited the location. Knowing once materials leave the private control of a person they are no longer subject to a search and seizure warrant, Dylhoff snapped on latex gloves, then opened the lid and began sifting through the contents. The detective hoped something inside the can would give him a clue to the disappearance of Khris Smith.

Assorted photos of people Dylhoff believed to be Khris and Lisa Smith were scattered among the debris. The photos, along with the negatives, had been cut into small pieces. Under the snapshots was a Nu-Vision prescription card in the name of Khristine Smith. It too had been cut. Dylhoff laid the pictures and health card aside as he picked up a letter verifying a Myrtle Beach reservation in Khris Smith's name. The last item Dylhoff found was a Portage Library notice instructing the missing woman to pick up a book.

Back at the station, the various items retrieved from the bin of food scraps, newspapers, vehicle parts, and an old oil filter and rags were tagged by Dylhoff and placed in the evidence bin at the Portage Police Department. Then he turned out his office light and closed the door for the evening. He had talked to several people and had made some interesting discoveries concerning the disappearance of Khris Smith.

Dylhoff was known as a persistent, hard-driving cop who went with his gut feelings about a case and didn't necessarily go by the book to find the answers to his probing questions. But as he drove off for the night, Dylhoff knew he was no closer to knowing where Khris was or what had happened to her than he had been at the beginning of the day.

Chapter 2

His second day on the Khris Smith case, Randy Dylhoff finally reached Khris's mother in Florida. Kay Klein provided little insight into the disappearance of her daughter. Klein hadn't spoken to Khris in over a month. She explained to Dylhoff that she and her daughter didn't share a close relationship. From the brief conversation with Klein, Dylhoff had some understanding of why Khris may have distanced herself from her mother. Klein expressed little concern for Khris or her whereabouts. The veteran cop sensed this had been common in the mother-daughter relationship.

"Khris and I have an acquaintance-type relationship," Klein said. "We aren't very close to each other. Khris tends to only tell her side of the story when anything goes wrong. It's always the other person's fault. She doesn't like rules and restrictions. While she was a teenager, she ran away from home numerous times."

Was that all to the Khris Smith disappearance? Had a rebellious teenager become a rebellious adult, reverting to an old pattern?

Klein continued, relating that Smith had told his mother-in-law that Khris had been arriving home with hickeys on her neck. He'd expressed disapproval of her male friends. None of Khris Smith's friends had mentioned the red blotches normally associated with young lovers in the throngs of newfound passion. Had they not noticed them, or were they a figment of Russ Smith's imagination?

"Russ told me Khris left him a letter stating she wanted to be with someone else and she was on her way to Florida. He said that's why he called me," Klein stated.

Klein again assured Dylhoff she hadn't heard from Khris and had no idea where she was or whom she might be with.

"Do you know if Khris was having an affair? That it could have been going on for approximately three months?" Dylhoff asked.

"I last talked to Khris about a month ago. She didn't say anything about an affair and she wouldn't tell me even if she were having one. She knows I wouldn't approve," Klein remarked. "They did have problems about two years ago, but I don't know of any recent troubles," Klein added. "More than anything, I'm very concerned that Khris left my granddaughter behind. She loves Lisa very much. I can't imagine she would just up and leave without taking Lisa with her. They are very close." There was a touch of distress in Klein's voice.

As Dylhoff set the receiver in the phone cradle on his desk, he glanced at the photo of Khris Smith, retrieved from the trash bin, among his reports. In the photo Khris Smith was smiling broadly. She wore shorts and a dark shirt with the word "Wow" in large letters across the front. It had obviously been taken in happier times. A nagging feeling continued to trouble him. The disappearance of Khris Smith just didn't add up to a runaway wife.

Later in the evening, on the same day Dylhoff first spoke with Kay Klein, she contacted him with additional information.

"Russ called again," Klein told Dylhoff. "He wanted to know what Khris had done to bring the cops into this. I never mentioned my conversation with you."

On the other end of the phone, Dylhoff's brow wrinkled and he scratched his chin. Was Smith upset that the police had been brought in to look into his wife's disappearance? If so, why? Wouldn't he be happy to have help finding his wife, to know she was safe? If not, why?

"I also talked to Lisa," Klein told him, her voice lifting slightly. "She seemed to be in a very good mood. She said she didn't want to go back home and she didn't want to go to school there anymore. Lisa made no mention of her mother. Nor did I."

Klein also revealed she had received a letter she had neglected to tell Dylhoff about in their previous conversation. The communication had been sent from Khris and was dated September 21, 1994, less than a week before her disappearance.

As Klein read the letter aloud to Dylhoff, it appeared that Khris had been in good spirits when she wrote it. Khris talked about her family and relatives living in Ohio. She ended by wishing her mother a happy birthday.

Twisting one end of his mustache, Dylhoff thought momentarily about the content and tone of Khris's letter. There was no mention of marital discord. No signs of depression. Yet, if Khris Smith was planning on leaving her family only days later, would her communication not have reflected some type of anguish concerning her decision? Some indication of her unhappiness? Dylhoff turned his attention back to Kay Klein's continuing comments.

"I'm worried about Khris. Russ said she took only

the bare essentials and some clothing. It's unlike her to just up and leave without taking her car or any of her other belongings," Klein said.

The veteran detective wondered if Khris Smith had taken her makeup. A woman seldom left without her makeup and personal products. They might leave behind many things, but, almost always, private items were packed and taken along.

"Khris has always been very nurturing," Klein continued. "Taking care of her home and family was her job for a number of years. This just doesn't make sense."

Over the next four days, Dylhoff and others with the Portage PD persisted in investigating the case that was quickly moving from a suspicious incident to a missing person. The Smith house was rechecked and appeared to be as secure as before. Nothing had noticeably changed. The only mail in the street-side white house-like mailbox with a green roof was a postcard from friends vacationing in Myrtle Beach.

To most of the outside world, it was life as usual in the Smith household.

As Kay Klein went about her daily routine of working and caring for her Florida home, the thought of Khris and her mysterious departure was never far from her mind. Klein and her daughter had shared a volatile relationship over the years, but she loved Khris and was now worried that something terrible might have happened to her only daughter. Klein began remembering recent conversations with her son-in-law. Talks that might somehow help the police find Khris. She phoned Detective Dylhoff again.

"I talked to Russ on Wednesday, September twenty-eighth, the day he claims Khris left," Klein stated. "He called to let me know that Khris had walked out on him.

He told me they had a terrible fight and that he needed to talk with her. He thought she might be coming down to Florida, to my house. If she did show up, he asked me to keep her here until he could get here to talk to her."

The story Klein told Dylhoff was not unlike the stories Smith had related to his neighbors, with one exception. Smith hadn't made mention of a fight with his wife the day she left. He had simply stated that when he arrived home, he'd found a note left by his wife informing him she was leaving him for another man. Just how "terrible" had the fight been? Dylhoff wondered.

"The first call I got from Russ was just after five P.M. I was still at work. The second call was later that night, around ten-thirty," Klein explained. "During the last call we had a short conversation. He was just checking to see whether or not Khris was here in Florida yet."

Klein had next heard from Russ two days later. He'd advised her he was in Dayton, Ohio, and had just called his house in Portage.

"He said Khris answered the phone at the house, so he was heading back to Portage," Klein said.

Dylhoff considered Klein's words. Smith had told him of the call as well, but he hadn't indicated he spoke with Khris, only that someone had picked up the receiver during his call. Had Smith actually spoken to his wife? Dylhoff made a mental note to ask Smith about the phone call, and the fight between him and his wife when they finally met face-to-face.

"Russ called my son, Troy, that same night," Klein continued, interrupting Dylhoff's thoughts.

Dylhoff jotted down a quick note, his next call would be to Klein's son.

* * *

"Yeah, I talked to Russ on Friday night, September thirtieth," Troy Klein told Dylhoff when contacted by the detective. "He called around nine or nine-thirty. He told me he was at his parents' house in Cridersville, Ohio."

"Did he say anything about Khris?" Dylhoff asked.

"He told me he and Khris had had an altercation two days earlier and he'd walked out on her. He said he left for an hour," Troy answered.

This was the second time Dylhoff had been told of a fight, or altercation as Troy called it, between Russ and Khris Smith.

"Russ also told me about a fight he and Khris had while living in Fort Wayne. Seems they got into a heated argument while in the car. Russ claimed Khris physically assaulted him and spit in his face. Russ stated he didn't do anything back to her. In fact, he said he could never physically hurt Khris," Troy reported.

Dylhoff scribbled a note on his desk pad, as he often did during phone interviews, and wondered why Smith would bring up an incident that happened more than two years earlier. And why was he so insistent that he could never hurt his wife physically? She had trampled his emotions by leaving him for another man, an experience that must have left Smith humiliated and angry. The question most prominent in Dylhoff's mind: how angry?

"He said he had to go back to work for an hour because one of his supervisors was coming in and there were some things that he had to get done," Troy continued. "After an hour at Sears, he went back home and Khris was gone. He didn't say where Lisa was."

Dylhoff wondered why Smith hadn't mentioned to his brother-in-law that Lisa had been in school and had been unaware of her mother's unexpected departure until her father informed her later in the day.

"Russ said he'd gotten as far as Lexington, Kentucky, when he called the house and Khris answered the phone. He told me he turned around and started back to Portage. When we talked, he said he was at his parents' house," Troy stated.

"Anything else you can remember?" Dylhoff asked.

"Yeah, he told me, even though he had been on vacation the whole week, there had been three different times when he had had to go into work for an hour or so because a Sears area supervisor was coming in," Troy answered.

"Is that the only time you've talked with Russ?" Dylhoff asked.

"No. He called again the next day. I answered the phone. It was about eight-thirty or nine in the morning. He said he was at his parents' house in Cridersville, Ohio," Troy told Dylhoff. "The conversation was short. Russ was angry. He wanted to know what Khris had done to draw the police into this. I told him the only thing I knew was that someone from the Portage Police Department had called and wanted to talk with Mom, but she wasn't home."

Dylhoff wrote down the time of the calls to Troy and Smith's alleged locations. He was preparing a timeline of Smith's activities and whereabouts, beginning with the morning he claimed Khris left for parts unknown.

Later that day, Dylhoff again spoke with Troy and Khris's mother, Kay Klein.

Klein stated she had called the Smith house in Portage the previous day and had reached the answering machine. The clear, upbeat voice of her daughter had rung in her ears. Klein had been relieved, believing that Khris was back home. But as she began to leave a message for Khris, Smith had picked up the phone.

"What terrible fight did you have with Khris? What was the fight about?" Klein had demanded.

"I caught Khris having an affair," Russ had answered calmly. "I told her to leave." Then Smith's voice began to change, anger creeping in as his words reverberated over the line. "I don't know who called the police or why they are involved in this," he said.

Klein had been surprised at Russ Smith's next words. "I've been to see an attorney and I've filed for divorce." Less than a week had passed since Khris had allegedly deserted her family, yet no one had heard a word from her.

Smith had also divulged to Klein that Khris had had an affair before, during Christmas 1992 while Klein was visiting for the holidays.

The memory of Khris standing in front of the Christmas tree she had meticulously decorated filled Klein's mind.

"She would put the kids in bed and make it look like we were all going to bed and everything was okay. Then she would sneak out of the house and come back in the morning before everybody got up. She even did it a couple of times while you were visiting at Christmas," Russ said.

Klein had had a hard time believing the things her son-in-law had said. But as she pondered his statement, Khris's words during Christmas 1992 rang in her ears.

"Russ and I might not be together very long. I'm starting to put things aside in preparation for the separation," Khris had said. She'd offered no further explanation.

The situation of her daughter's unexplained disappearance troubled Klein. The events described by her son-in-law made little sense. But most troubling of all was a strange, repeated plea made by Smith to his mother-in-law.

"Please promise me you won't desert Lisa."

Chapter 3

While waiting for Russ Smith to arrive back in Michigan, Dylhoff began scrutinizing the lives of both Russ and Khristine Smith. Information about each of them, as well as their relationship as a couple, would be beneficial in helping to piece together events that led up to Khris's mysterious departure.

Russell Smith was born May 20, 1962, to middle-class parents in Cridersville, Ohio. His father, Roger, the dominant parent in the Smith household, worked for the Dana Corporation, while his mother, Linda, was a stay-at-home mom to the four Smith children. Russell, who became known as "Rusty" because of his reddish hair, was the second of three sons. He also had a younger sister.

The Smiths lived a simple life in a town of twenty-one hundred people. Their modest home was situated on a quiet street, across from the local funeral home and crematory.

During high school Smith was an overweight, knock-kneed teen who was an average student. His classmates remembered him as being "okay," someone who never stood out in the crowd. After high school graduation, Smith attended a technical school for two years. He then began an automotive career, which eventually took him to his position as Sears Automotive Center manager in Portage, Michigan.

His job and one-hundred-pound weight loss from his high school weight of three hundred appeared to have given him newfound confidence. He was handsome, dressed neatly, and walked with a cocky air of self-assuredness. Smith appeared to have the personality, potential, and work ethic to go far.

Russ Smith met a young woman named Lucia. No one was certain if it was love or lust that prompted Smith to propose. They were both young, too young to take on the responsibilities of marriage. Although he thought Lucia was a really nice girl, when Khris Klein walked into the Sears store where he was working, he found any thoughts of his young wife had dimmed.

Khris Klein was very pretty and alluring in a way Lucia wasn't. When she strolled into the Sears store, she told Smith she was having a headlight problem. She needed a special star screwdriver to replace the lamp. He handed her his screwdriver and watched with keen interest as she walked toward her car, bent down, and began working on the headlight. In the process, Khris apparently removed the adjustment screws and the headlamp nearly fell out. Smith eagerly helped her make the repair, refusing to charge for his labor.

Khris had offered to take a couple of the other mechanics out for pizza and Smith was included. Smith and Khris hit it off immediately. That was the beginning of the end of his marriage to Lucia.

For years Russell Smith had been enthralled with police work. He opted to become one of three part-time officers on the Cridersville Police Department. He had lived in the community for most of his life and had a strong interest in being a police officer.

Most of those positions were filled with people known to someone already on the force. Smith just walked in, filled out an application, and was accepted because of his years in the community.

Like other part-time officers, Smith worked from 5:00 P.M. to 10:00 at night, and rotated through weekends. Roger Rhodes, the chief of police in Cridersville, considered Smith an average officer, not the best, but not the worst either. There had been no complaints made against Smith and he appeared to be even-tempered and laid-back. Nothing seemed to rattle Smith or get him stirred up. His fellow officers considered him a loner. He shared a close relationship with no one at the department.

One of Smith's fellow officers had been seeing Khris Klein prior to Smith's involvement with her. Doug Vermillion had ended the short-term relationship when warned by his brother that Khris was not necessarily looking for marriage, but that she wanted a child very much. In addition, a friend of Vermillion's had told him that Khris, who lived with the friend and his wife at the time to help care for their children, had been scantily dressed in sexy clothes several times when his wife was not at home. He told Vermillion that he would go to his workshop and wait for his wife to get home, fearful of what might happen if he remained in the residence.

Vermillion himself had observed Khris in her driveway, washing her car in sexually revealing attire. Khris definitely gave the impression of being a loose woman on the prowl.

As Smith's contact with Khris became more frequent, his marriage to Lucia continued to crumble. On April 30, 1986, the couple was granted an uncontested divorce. The major part of the settlement agreement pertained to the house the couple had purchased

together in Cridersville. Russ agreed to quick claim any
and all interest he had in the property to Lucia.

Russ Smith was free. Free to marry Khristine Klein.

Unlike Russ Smith, Khristine Klein had a far less stable upbringing. She was born December 17, 1966, to
Kay and Harry Klein. When Khris was very young, her
parents divorced, her father leaving his young family
behind. Perhaps his departure so early in her life is
what left Khris needing, craving, the attention of men.
Her relationship with her mother wasn't good.

Kay Klein attributed the breach in their relationship to Khris's rebellious streak, but perhaps Khris
thought life on the streets would be better than life
without a father and with a mother who was less than
nurturing.

Perhaps because of her chaotic home life, Khris developed the fine art of flirtation and combined it with
seductive and revealing clothing to produce an irre-
sistible allure for men. It was an appeal that got her
into trouble, even as a teenager.

Khristine Klein became pregnant in her teens.
Unmarried and five months into the ill-conceived
pregnancy, Kay Klein drove her daughter to Cincin-
nati for an abortion.

It was a two-day hardship. The first day Khris en-
dured a procedure that snuffed out the life growing
inside her swollen womb. It was a traumatic ordeal, as
Khris had felt the baby kick. She cried for the procedure to stop. She wanted her baby to live, but it was
too late. The procedure couldn't be reversed. There
was no further movement. The second day the child
that was never-to-be was sucked from Khris's body. It

was an experience Khris Klein would never forget. She vowed never again.

Khris Klein and Russell Smith were wed on November 13, 1986. They appeared to be the perfect couple. Russ was introverted, where Khris was outgoing and vivacious. The two complemented one another well.

Khris had ignored her teenage vow and was pregnant with their first child at the time of their marriage. Khris was going to have the child she always wanted and Russ would be a first-time father. He and Lucia had never had children; he was delighted to be having a child with Khris.

The few months Khris and Russ were married prior to Lisa's birth were wonderful. They seemed to be on their way to a long and happy union, but the birth of Lisa changed Khris. At first, Khris was furious that her firstborn child was a girl and not a boy. For a while she seemed to turn her fury on Russ. He felt as though he couldn't do anything right or anything that would please her.

A short time after Lisa was born, Khris returned to the hospital and had her tubes tied. She had the child she wanted; no others were needed.

In time Khris became a good homemaker and a dedicated mother. She took pride in her home, often being accused by others of being a perfectionist. Even the recipe box in the kitchen held typed recipe cards, with each food category on a different color card. She was viewed by friends as a good wife, great mother, and a caring friend. Khris often sent thoughtful notes to friends, occasionally clipping out a news article they might find of interest.

Russ, on the other hand, was described as quiet and standoffish. Outward appearances portrayed a loving husband and devoted father, but he had few close friends. After marrying Khris, Russ had even pulled away from his close-knit family.

On August 18, 1994, both Russ and Khris Smith had sought testing, each feeling they had some type of attention deficit disorder (ADD). Khris was found to have none. She indicated that her marriage was primarily stable, but sometimes rocky. Khris expressed a good relationship with Lisa, although they were experiencing some power struggles. She was referred to a psychologist for the rocky marriage and problems with her daughter; however, she never followed up.

A month after Khris disappeared, Russ sought the services of a psychologist. He had been diagnosed earlier with ADD, and within two months was dealing with neurotic depression.

The perfect marriage that everyone had envied seemed to have ended abruptly and with traumatic results.

Chapter 4

Dylhoff made his way to the front steps of the Smith house on Thunderbay. The house was illuminated by a single porch light. At 9:30 P.M., four days after Smith had informed his neighbors that Khris had left him, Dylhoff pushed Smith's doorbell.

"Russ Smith?" Dylhoff asked.

"Yes," Smith said, his brow wrinkled in a questioning glare.

"I'm Detective Randy Dylhoff. We spoke on the phone," Dylhoff said. "I'm here about your wife. I've been in contact with her mother, Kay Klein. I'd like to talk to you."

Smith opened the front door, inviting the police detective inside.

As Dylhoff stepped on the checkered parquet entry, he noticed double louvered doors directly in front of him. To his right was a straight staircase, which turned at a ninety-degree left angle after a small landing. A wooden banister had been added to aid in the ascent and descent of the wooden steps. A small octagonal-shaped window was to the right of the front door.

As Dylhoff followed Smith into the family's living room, he noticed two paperback books on a shelf: *Corpus Delicti* and *A Rose for Her Grave*. Dylhoff was curious about the books with such ominous titles and wondered which of the Smiths had been reading the true crime works.

Even with the absence of Khris Smith, the detective could feel her presence. From the handmade wreaths that adorned the walls, the soft pastel colors that accented an otherwise plain room, and a photo album on display that was surely assembled by the loving hands of a woman, Dylhoff knew it was Khris who had taken pride in decorating the Smith home.

"What can you tell me about your wife's leaving?" Dylhoff asked.

"A disagreement, a misunderstanding, really, between us, started on Saturday, September twenty-fourth. The three of us—Khris, Lisa, and I—had gone to my sister's wedding in Cridersville, Ohio. While we were there, Khris didn't want to get in any of the family pictures," Smith explained. "She insisted we sit in the back of the auditorium during the wedding, rather than in the front with the family. She was just being a real bitch."

Dylhoff watched Smith with interest. He was a large man, six feet one, around two hundred pounds. Like Dylhoff, the only facial hair Smith had was a mustache. Smith's was brownish red, lightly sprinkled with gray.

"Things were going so bad we didn't stick around very long after the wedding reception. We headed back home to Portage." Then, with a hint of hurt mixed with irritation, Smith said, "On the way back, Khris was talking about how unhappy she was. That she wanted to change her name back to her maiden name."

"How long did the disagreement, as you call it, continue?" Dylhoff asked, urging Smith to go on.

"Things were okay on Sunday and Monday. On Tuesday night, the night before she left, the three of us—Khris, Lisa, and I—went to the Wings hockey game. The Wings played the Cleveland Lumberjacks," Smith said with a slight smile. "Then on the way back home, Khris began taking potshots at me."

"What do you mean, 'potshots'?" Dylhoff queried.

"Just nit-picking little things about me, about our relationship," Smith said with sarcasm.

"Do you remember anything in particular?" Dylhoff asked.

"One thing comes to mind. She was commenting on her wedding ring. Lisa asked me how much it cost. Khris made the smart-aleck comment, 'Well, it was either not enough, or too much; which one was it, Russ?'" Smith spoke with thinly veiled resentment and embarrassment. "There was no way to win, not against a statement like that."

"How were things between you on Wednesday, September twenty-eighth, the day she left?" Dylhoff inquired.

"We got up. I took Lisa out to the bus stop; then I came back in the house. That's when Khris handed me a three-page letter," Smith said, handing over three handwritten pages on lined paper to Dylhoff.

The experienced detective studied the pages before reading. There was no date at the top of the first page and no date or signature at the end of the third. The letter was tidy with the exception of the last two lines. Mark-outs depicted signs of stress or confusion. Dylhoff read the letter as Smith watched.

The letter began simply, "Russ." She wrote of her own personal needs getting lost as she attempted to watch out for the feelings of everyone else in her life. She expressed a desire to date, to come and go as she pleased, making reference to an agreement that she and her husband had apparently made concerning her need for time and space. But Khris's desire for time apart from Russ seemed hindered by notes he'd left for her and his expressions of love. It was obvious to Detective Dylhoff that Khris Smith wanted time alone. She indicated her husband's lack of attention as a reason for her decision to leave him. She even appeared bitter when she wrote that she hadn't seemed important enough to him so she guessed now he wasn't important enough to her.

As Dylhoff read on, he was surprised to see that Khris had indicated in her letter that she intended to stay in the home the Smiths had made together while she was pursuing an independent life. The statement was even more surprising after noting that Khris Smith admitted that another man had influenced her decision to "move on," although she insisted that she was making the move on her own.

Khris Smith's letter rambled toward the end, talking of the various roles of men and women. But the last sentenced seemed to sum up Khris Smith's confusion. She was in love with two men and one child, all in different ways.

The letter ended abruptly, as if Khris Smith hadn't finished. Had she not had time to complete her message to her husband, or had she been interrupted?

Dylhoff, holding the pages in his hands, asked Smith, "Can I keep these?"

"No. You can make a copy, but I want to keep the originals," Smith answered.

"What happened after Khris gave you the letter?" Dylhoff asked.

"She went upstairs to take a shower. After reading the letter, I got angry and went upstairs. Khris and I got into an argument. She was making comments about how I was not there for her and she needed me. I told her I wanted her out and I left the house to cool down," Smith said angrily.

"How long were you gone?" Dylhoff questioned.

"About one or two hours. When I got back I found Khris had, in fact, left," Smith replied, his anger having subsided.

When asked what items his wife had taken with her, Smith said she had taken personal hygiene items, makeup, basic clothes, and shoes. Two suitcases were missing, one about five cubic feet and the other one smaller, fitting inside the larger.

"Why didn't she take her car?" Dylhoff inquired.

"When I went out, I pulled the coil wire off her car so she couldn't take it," he responded smugly.

Smith told Dylhoff that when he got home and found Khris gone, he was afraid she was at the school to take Lisa with her.

"I went to the school and directly to her classroom, without stopping at the office," Smith explained. "I just looked in the window and saw Lisa was there. It was just before lunch, about eleven o'clock. When I left the school, I went to work and told my boss, the main store manager, that I was having some family problems. Then I headed back to the school to talk with Lisa's teacher. It was probably twelve-thirty then. I advised Mrs. Warren that we were having family problems and I would be taking Lisa out of school for the rest of that week and the following week."

Smith claimed that during his heated conversation with Khris, she had told him she thought she might head to Florida to her mother's house. He decided to drop Lisa at his parents' in Ohio, then head for Florida himself.

"I decided to go there because I wanted to talk with Khris. I wanted to try to work things out," he explained.

Smith's words were contradictory. First he told Khris he wanted her to leave, but then he said he was willing to travel to Florida to work things out.

Smith claimed he had left Cridersville, just off Interstate Highway 75, several hundred miles south of Toledo, and set out for Florida.

"I stopped several times at different locations on the way down to Florida and called back home to Portage. I wanted to see if Khris had returned and whether or not she would answer the phone," Smith explained.

"I used a calling card at different pay phones. When I got to Lexington, Kentucky, about six A.M., Thursday morning, someone answered the phone at home," Smith reported. "I can't remember if they said hello or if I said hello first, but they hung up immediately. I don't think they said anything. I just assumed it was Khris."

"What did you do then?" Dylhoff asked.

Smith explained that he called his mom from the same pay phone in Lexington, advising her he thought Khris was back home. He had then informed his mother he was headed back to Portage.

"I also called Kay, Khris's mom, and told her about the phone call and that I believed Khris had picked up the receiver," Smith replied. "I told her I was going back home."

Smith couldn't remember what time he had called Kay Klein, or from where he had made the call. He did remember arriving in Portage about 3:00 or 4:00 that afternoon.

From where Dylhoff was seated, he could see a cheery dining room furnished with sturdy oak furniture and a chandelier centered over the table. The walls of the breakfast room had been painted hunter green, with curtains and a table runner with the same green accents.

"When I got in the house, I found the garage-door opener and Khris's wedding ring on the kitchen table. She had cut the ring off. She'd gained a little weight and was unable to slip it off," Smith explained.

"What about keys to the house and the car?" Dylhoff asked.

"She didn't take her set of keys with her when she left the first time," Smith said.

Dylhoff thought about Smith's answer and wondered how Khris got back in the house. Nothing looked disturbed and Smith said nothing had been taken from the residence. The Smith home appeared to be as pristine as described to him by neighbors, friends, and family.

"On Thursday night or Friday morning, I went back to my parents' house. On Monday I contacted an attorney to file for divorce," Smith continued.

"Why file for divorce so soon?" Dylhoff asked, calculating that his wife had been gone only five days at that time. "Khris may be coming back."

Smith defended his actions, stating he felt strongly that his wife was having an affair and that it had become even more obvious by what she had written in her letter. Smith claimed that Khris's own mother advised him that while they were living in Lima, Ohio, Khris was having an affair then.

"Kay stopped by the house one day and Khris had some guy there, who apparently was a shoe salesman in the local PicWay Shoes. I realize now why the guy was so friendly with her when she was in the store, and why she always liked to shop there for shoes," Smith said.

"Then there was the affair with that guy named Lyn. They met at Lisa's dance school, where his daughter took lessons at the same time," Smith added.

"How do you know she was having an affair?" Dylhoff questioned, realizing that Kay Klein had already denied any liaison between Khris and Lyn and Lyn flatly refuted the allegation.

"Khris would put Lisa to bed, and then within an hour or so after that, Khris would get up and say she was leaving, that she was going to Lyn's. She'd tell me she'd be back before Lisa got up. This would happen a couple of times a week. She even took my Sears charge card and bought a negligee she kept at his house," Smith said, his resentment obvious.

"How do you know that?" Dylhoff asked, curious to know why a man would put up with such blatant behavior by his wife.

"When the affair was over, she brought the negligee and her personal items back to this house," Smith said.

"Did you ever follow her?" Dylhoff inquired.

"No. I didn't have to. I knew where she was going because she told me," Smith responded matter-of-factly. "She had made comments in the past about leaving," Smith continued. "About leaving Lisa and never coming back."

As the conversation continued, Dylhoff learned that Khris Smith had taken no credit cards with her and no checkbook. Smith knew this, he said, because they remained in a household lockbox, where Khris had put the cards after having her purse stolen sometime earlier. Khris did have a cash-withdrawal card for their checking and savings accounts, but Smith had checked with the bank and no withdrawals had been made.

Dylhoff couldn't help but wonder about Khris Smith. Her outward appearance was that of a woman concerned with her home, her daughter, and herself. She maintained them all in meticulous fashion. Why, then, would a woman like Khris Smith, a woman who took pride in all she did, suddenly leave it all behind? Surely she would have taken something from her marriage with Smith. Even if she had left for another man, would she not have taken money? Money she herself had earned. She had expressed to friends her need for independence. Why leave one relationship based on total reliance for another? And the biggest question of all loomed over Khris Smith's disappearance like a mist in early morning. Why would a loving, devoted, and overprotective mother leave her child?

These were all questions that would have no answers until Khris Smith was found.

Chapter 5

It was difficult to determine who was the dominant force in the Smith family. While Kay Klein insisted that Khris "ruled the roost," Debbie Orosz contended that, from her perspective, it was Russ Smith who made the rules, and Khris who obediently followed them.

Kay Klein characterized her daughter as a woman who always did what she wanted and didn't care whom it affected. Klein had even blamed Smith in part for her daughter's selfish behavior, accusing him of failing to challenge Khris for the way she acted. Yet Debbie Orosz portrayed her neighbor as someone who feared her husband. She said Khris would rush home, regardless of what she was doing, to be there when Smith arrived, or face possible retribution. According to Orosz, Smith even restricted his wife's food intake so she would lose weight.

"Khris came over, and while we were talking, Khris was commenting on how she felt weak and dizzy. I asked what was going on and she said Russ thought she was too fat, so she was on a diet. I asked her if she had told Russ how she was feeling and she said his only comment was 'Why don't you just go have another glass of water; that'll fill you up.' Then Khris broke down and started crying. She made comments like 'Doesn't he care about me?'" Debbie had told Dylhoff.

In the photos Dylhoff had retrieved from the Smiths' garbage can, he had noted a slim, attractive woman, not an overweight female.

The detective learned that Russ Smith was married when he first met Khris and that Khris felt her in-laws had never accepted her, believing she had broken up his first marriage. Orosz also talked about how Khris thought Russ had bugged the phone because she could hear different clicks while she was talking. Debbie depicted Khris as paranoid and scared of her husband.

Both Khris and Russ appeared to be individuals with serious personal problems. Often, when two such people marry, it is inevitable that it will be a very disturbed, often hateful union.

Dylhoff was beginning to get a sense of the true relationship between Khris and Russ Smith. Although seemingly perfect on the outside, the Smith marriage was filled with unhappiness, distrust, and volatility. It appeared the fantasies of both Khris and Russ were repeatedly pierced, causing them to be increasingly alienated from one another. It seemed the major factor in the deterioration of their marriage was that neither of them could possibly be as perfect as the other had expected. To outsiders, it looked as if Khris had tried to be as ideal a wife as her husband had wanted her to be. Within two days of moving into the house on Thunderbay, Khris had everything unpacked, had even had pictures hung on the walls. But keeping up the pace of perfection seemed to have taken its toll on Khris. Over time her love had apparently turned to resentment.

Because of her own troubled childhood, Khris Smith wanted a better life for her daughter than the one she had experienced growing up. "The two were inseparable and always did things together," Debbie told

Dylhoff. "Khris has probably done more with Lisa in the last couple of years than I have with my own kids."

If Khris Smith wanted more for Lisa, wanted her to have what she considered a wonderful childhood, why, then, did she leave her behind? That was the one question that continued to fester in Dylhoff's mind.

The fact remained, Khris Smith was gone. There was no trail of evidence leading to her whereabouts. No secret love nest. Khris Smith had vanished without a trace.

On October 7, 1994, nine days after her unexpected departure, Khristine Renee Smith was officially entered into the National Crime Information Computer (NCIC) as a missing person.

The fall leaves had turned to hues of yellow, orange, and brilliant red. The air was crisp and the wind biting as Dylhoff drove to the home of Rick and Charlene Lemons. The Lemonses had been friends with the Smiths since the Smiths arrived in Portage. They originally met through school; the Lemonses' son and Lisa Smith were classmates.

"We've done numerous social and family outings over the time we've known them," Rick Lemons said of the Smiths. "Russ seemed like a very caring and considerate husband. We thought he treated Khris very well. Russ and I went out together on different fishing expeditions, anywhere from an overnight trip to two or three days. Russ always called home every day to see how things were going with Khris and Lisa."

The last major outing the Lemonses and the Smiths had was in July 1993, which was a three-day fishing trip on Lake Erie. They had talked by phone on later occasions in an attempt to set up another excursion.

"On Thursday, September twenty-ninth, Russ stopped by," Charlene Lemons told Dylhoff, speaking of the night following Khris Smith's disappearance. "He asked if I'd seen Khris. I thought he was talking about that night, so I told him no. Then he told me she'd moved out. He pulled a multipage letter out of his pocket and handed it to me. He told me to read it. I asked him if he was sure he wanted me to, and he said I might as well know it all."

Charlene Lemons had gotten the impression from Smith that his wife had had one fling after another with different men. Khris had never mentioned another man or an affair, but Charlene did recall a conversation she had with Khris on Memorial Day weekend in May 1993.

The two families had been on a jaunt. She and Khris had an opportunity for a private talk. That's when Khris stated she was unhappy with the situation between her and Russ and the role she had to play. Khris indicated that it seemed all she did was get Russ up and off to work, get Lisa off to school, and she felt that this role was causing her to lose her identity. Then again in July, she'd made reference to being unhappy with her relationship.

"She also talked about how she didn't care for having sex with Russ," Charlene told the detective. "It seemed like every time they had intercourse, the very next day, she got some type of vaginal infection. She thought that she was allergic to Russ. She stated she preferred abstinence in their relationship; however, it was not Russ's preference. She said she got infections so frequently and so bad that Russ had gone to the doctor and was taking medication to see if there was something that he had that was causing the problem. It hadn't helped."

Had Khris Smith's medical problems caused her husband to retaliate against her? And if she had so many problems with intercourse, would she have been having an affair? Dylhoff wanted to know if either of the Lemonses had ever seen Smith abuse his wife, or if Khris had shared any abusive experiences with them.

Charlene could only recall one incident when Russ Smith seemed to have lost it emotionally. It was Lisa's sixth birthday party, but Khris hadn't been the target of his anger. It had been his daughter.

Lisa was passing out forks to her young friends, who were anxiously awaiting birthday cake topped with ice cream, when Russ yelled, "Give me the goddamn fork!" Charlene remembered that Khris had been embarrassed by her husband's harsh words. She'd lowered her head and shaken it side to side, her short brown hair swinging softly.

Rick had only one thing to add on the subject of Russ Smith's temperament.

"Russ said he was so angry when he found out Khris left that he put his fist through the bathroom wall. He also talked about how he had damaged the bathtub and shower enclosure and had to replace them. He assured me he never hit Khris, and never would," Rick reported.

Dylhoff listened with renewed interest. This was the first time he'd heard that rage had welled up in Russ Smith at learning of his wife's departure. The first indication that his anger had led to any form of physical action.

Neither Charlene nor Rick Lemons could think of where Khris could be or with whom. But one comment, spoken offhandedly, took Dylhoff by surprise.

"She made the comment one time that she needed

to break her bad habit of picking up hitchhikers. Apparently she felt sorry for them or something and would pick them up if she saw them along the road," Charlene said.

The hitchhiker story provided an entirely new angle to the case. Was it possible that Khris Smith had left her husband to meet a lover, picked up a stranger, and something had happened to her from that point? When he tried to surmise what vehicle she would have used, the scenario seemed unlikely.

As with Kay Klein, the Husses, and the Oroszes, Smith had told the Lemonses how he had started for Florida only to turn back when he called home and Khris supposedly picked up the phone.

The Lemonses hadn't seen or heard from Russ Smith since September 29.

Detective Dylhoff received a call from Harry Klein Jr., Khris's father. Klein had talked to Russ Smith, who, in Klein's opinion, hadn't seemed very concerned about Khris being missing. Klein wanted to know what had to be done to file a missing persons report. Dylhoff assured him that a report had already been filed and he had been officially assigned the missing persons case.

Russ Smith seemed to be one step ahead of Dylhoff all through the investigation. When Dylhoff made contact with Linda Kelder, director of KinderCare, Russ Smith had already been there. He had visited the children's facility on September 28, the day his wife allegedly disappeared, at three o'clock in the afternoon. Smith had asked if Khris had been at work, then advised Kelder that he and Khris were having marital difficulties. He even told his wife's employer that Khris had admitted she was seeing another man, and that that wasn't the first time something like that had happened.

It looked as if Russ Smith was telling everyone who knew him or who knew Khris that not only had she left him, but she'd left him for another man. Would most men share the facts of their wives' abandonment, or would they conceal the information that they had been left for someone their spouses deemed more appealing? It seemed like a giant blow to any man's ego. To answer those questions, Dylhoff would have to get to know Smith far better.

On October 10, with the fall leaves fluttering to the ground, Detective Dylhoff made a second visit to Russ Smith at his residence on Thunderbay. He parked his car by the curb, next to the green-and-white mailbox, the address numbers prominently placed in a vertical arrangement down the wooden post that held the box securely in place in the center of a rock garden bed.

"Have you had any contact with Khris?" Dylhoff asked Smith once inside the residence.

"No," Smith replied.

"Do you have any body X rays of Khris?" Dylhoff asked. Smith knew if a body that met the general description of his wife was found, X rays would be useful in the final identification.

"No," Smith said.

"Was Khris ever fingerprinted?" Dylhoff continued.

"Not as far as I know, not as an adult. But I think she got into some trouble as a juvenile. Her mother would probably know something about that," Smith said, adding another blemish to his wife's character.

Smith offered the name of Khris's doctor and dentist as well as their addresses. They too could possibly be useful in identifying any remains of Khris Smith in the event that she had met with foul play—a possibility that Dylhoff wasn't yet ready to accept as fact.

Smith advised the detective that he had contacted all the credit card companies and closed the accounts. He also had checked with Standard Federal Bank, where the couple had a checking account, but no money transactions had been processed.

"Did Khris have access to any other funds?" Dylhoff asked.

"No, not that I know of. I did get a phone call on Saturday when I got back from Ohio. A lady was calling about an ad in the paper for a sewing machine. Evidently, Khris had placed an ad in the paper to sell her sewing machine, but she hadn't mentioned anything about it to me. The lady came over and looked at the machine and bought it," Smith said, adding that Khris often ran ads in the newspaper to sell various items. But would she have placed the ad knowing she wouldn't be there to complete any sale? Dylhoff wondered.

Smith also provided the name of an attorney he had used two years earlier for divorce proceedings. Smith claimed Khris had refused to sign the documents and ultimately the divorce action had been dropped.

The divorce petition had been initiated as a result of the affair Russ Smith was convinced had been happening between Khris and her friend Lyn. Smith insisted that Khris had kept personal items at the man's house; then when the affair was over, she'd brought them home. Those items included makeup, a robe, and lingerie. As before, Smith stated that Khris would leave after she put Lisa to bed and would come back in the morning before Lisa got up.

If Lyn had told Dylhoff the truth and there had

been no affair with Smith's wife, then Khris's night-time activity could be explained easily by her friends. They had characterized Khris as a woman who didn't care for crowds, frequently shopping at the local twenty-four-hour store after putting Lisa to bed.

Smith claimed the relationship between Khris and Lyn declined when Smith took his wife out to teach her how to drive a standard-shift vehicle. He talked of the fun he and Khris had, the laughter they shared at her inability to shift without jerking or stalling out. When the couple arrived home, the phone had rung and Smith said he believed it had been a call from Lyn. Smith claimed Lyn had become angry with Khris when he learned the Smiths had spent the day driving. Presumably, Lyn had been jealous that he had not had the pleasure of taking Khris out himself. "That was the beginning of the end of the relationship," Smith said, a slight smirk on his face.

"I've contacted a number of your neighbors to find out if they happened to see anything unusual the day Khris left," Dylhoff said, watching Smith closely for any reaction. "I'll be contacting others. Someone mentioned seeing a red pickup truck near the house on the Wednesday she left and a man about your size. Do you know anyone with a red truck?"

"No, I don't," Smith replied.

"I'm told when you left to go to Ohio you had several large items in the back of your truck. A cage-type thing and some other items," Dylhoff prodded.

"The cage was Lisa's rabbit cage. I took it to Ohio. There was also a bicycle and a large garbage can in the truck," Smith said.

"What was in the garbage can?" Dylhoff asked.

"Khris's clothes. I put them in the barrel and was

going to take them to her in Florida. I brought them back on the truck and put them in the basement," Smith said.

"What kind of garbage can was it?" Dylhoff asked.

"It was a large black barrel," Smith answered.

Her mother had been missing just over a week when Russ Smith traveled to Ohio and brought his daughter back to Portage with him. They were living alone in the house on Thunderbay. Smith would see Lisa off to school each morning, then pick her up every afternoon, taking her back to Sears with him while he finished his workday. He was trying to set up Saturday arrangements since he had to work, but he was having difficulty in finding suitable care for the seven-year-old.

Lisa was not unfamiliar with the Sears store. As a younger child she had been taken to the automotive section each night while her parents painted the shop. Russ was the new manager and wanted his area to be sharp-looking. He had convinced Khris to help him paint as Lisa lay bundled in the backseat of their car, sleeping. The car, parked inside one of the service bays, was safe. The arrangement allowed Khris and Russ the time needed to spruce up the area. Lisa had been oblivious to the hard work and laughter of her parents as they spread the blue paint on the walls and, occasionally, on each other.

Remembering the good times with Khris, Smith telephoned Kay Klein in Florida.

"I'm feeling lonely. I miss Khris," Smith told his mother-in-law, depression marring his words. "I don't know how you do it. And I don't know how you did it on your own, raising children."

Russ Smith was obviously feeling the pain of a lost partner and the stress of being a single parent responsible for the life of a seven-year-old child. He had big shoes to fill. Khris had been the perfect mother, if not the perfect wife.

Chapter 6

Russ Smith was considered a conscientious employee. During June and July 1994, two months prior to his wife's disappearance, he had been chosen to fill in for the district business manager of the auto department. During that time Smith covered twenty-one stores in the West Michigan area, from Traverse City, north to Lima, Ohio, and south, including the Jackson, Michigan, area as well as Fort Wayne, Indiana. The assignment required him to stay overnight numerous times, sometimes as long as a week.

When Smith completed the two-month assignment in September 1994, he requested a two-week vacation, telling the main store manager, Don Sewell, that he planned to spend time with his mother-in-law in Florida. However, he changed his plans when his wife's grandmother became ill. The family decided to meet in Ohio instead.

On the day Khris Smith disappeared, Sewell was interviewing a prospective employee in his office when there was a knock at the door. It was Russ Smith.

When Sewell completed his interview and Russ Smith sat in the chair across from his supervisor's desk, Sewell first learned Khris Smith had left her family. Smith handed Swell Khris's three-page letter written on yellow legal-size paper.

"Are you sure you want me to read it?" Sewell asked, believing it was too personal to share with others.

"Yes, I want you to know what's going on," Smith replied.

Sewell quickly read through Khris's letter, then Russ asked what he should do now that Khris was gone.

"How do you feel about the whole situation?" Sewell asked.

"I want to keep my family together and I don't want Khris to leave," Smith stated, his voice breaking. Smith's eyes were red and he appeared to have been crying, even before arriving at Sewell's office.

Sewell advised his employee that, if he really wanted to keep his family unified, when he did talk to Khris, he would have to control his emotions. "Don't get angry or upset, try to talk things through with her," Sewell advised.

Sewell gave Smith information on the company employee-assistance program, a plan that would provide no-cost marital counseling for the Smiths.

"Is there anything I can do?" Sewell asked.

Smith requested the following week off, and Sewell complied. The Sears manager had heard the Smiths had experienced marital problems before, although it had always been hard for him to believe. At store parties they always appeared to be happy. If Smith needed an additional week off to find Khris and try to work things out, he was glad to oblige.

Detective Dylhoff was anxious to talk with Lisa Smith. Russ Smith had indicated it would be no problem, yet when Dylhoff arrived at the Smith house on October 13, two weeks after Dylhoff had received the assignment of looking into Khris Smith's disappearance, Smith advised him that he had contacted a child psychologist.

"The psychologist recommended that you not talk with Lisa about Khris leaving," Smith stated. "After you left here yesterday, I told Lisa you wanted to come back and talk with her. She became very upset.

"She said, 'Please, Daddy, I don't want to talk to him. Please don't make me talk to him.' She hasn't said much about her mother leaving and doesn't want to talk to anyone about it."

Smith indicated he had contacted a local counselor who had worked with Lisa a year before when the Smiths believed the child was showing signs of attention deficit disorder.

Dylhoff was disappointed that he would not be allowed to talk to Lisa Smith. He believed she might have information unknown to others about her mother. Dylhoff knew he would have to wait.

Before leaving Smith, Dylhoff asked him again about the items seen in the back of his truck when he was departing Portage for Ohio. Smith again described the cage as that belonging to Lisa for her rabbit, the child's bike, and the barrel, which contained Khris's clothes.

"The barrel is still in the basement," Smith advised.

"Do you mind if I take a look at it?" Dylhoff asked.

Smith led Dylhoff down a flight of stairs leading to the basement. Dylhoff walked to a large, round green plastic garbage can with a black top. As he lifted the lid, Dylhoff found women's clothes inside, just as Smith had described. A black fifty-five-gallon barrel was nearby, but empty. A circular stain, the size of the barrel bottom, was close by.

"The clothes I had put in there, I threw out," Smith informed Dylhoff.

The barrel was dry and clean inside. It appeared to be new, with no liquid or anything else having been stored inside to soil it.

"Where did you get the barrel?" Dylhoff asked.

"From a deliveryman at work," Smith said.

Dylhoff took the opportunity to take in the interior of the basement, including the contents. There were two clothes racks, an ironing board and iron, and shelves filled with books, games, and aerosol cans. He noticed a large, long tanning bed. One of the Smiths' neighbors had mentioned the tanning bed in their statement as one of Khris Smith's most prized possessions. The missing woman had enjoyed spending time in the unit, tanning her skin to a golden brown. Would she miss the bed enough to come back for it? Or could she?

The inquiry, now turned investigation, went as most missing persons cases go. Dylhoff talked to as many people as possible in an effort to gain any information that would lead to the whereabouts of Khris Smith.

Garneta Titas, Khris Smith's aunt, told the detective that Khris's grandmother, in poor heath, was now living with her. The grandmother had vacated her home in Lafayette, Ohio, but they had made a point of keeping an eye on the property, especially since Khris knew where the extra key to the house was kept.

"We haven't heard from Khris or seen any sign of her being in the area," Titas told Dylhoff.

Titas described her niece as a strong-willed woman with a mind of her own. She revealed that six years prior, when the Smiths were living in Lima, Ohio, Khris had had a boyfriend. She was unaware if Khris had continued the relationship after moving from Lima.

As Dylhoff was running down his list of people to interview, he received a call from Don Sewell. The Sears manager asked to speak to the detective again concerning Russ Smith.

"There's something that's been bothering me," Sewell began, nervousness threading through his words. "When we talked before, I failed to mention Russ and his guns."

Dylhoff listened closely. This was the second reference made during the investigation concerning Russ Smith's gun collection.

"The Monday following Khris's disappearance, Russ asked if I would mind storing his guns for a couple of days. Russ said he had no idea who had access to his house or who Khris had taken off with, so he wanted to get the guns out of the house. He said it would just be for a couple of days because he was going back to Ohio to pick up his daughter."

Smith had dropped the firearms off that day, five days after Khris left, and picked them up three days later. Smith had informed Sewell he was taking the gun collection to his parents' home.

The gun assemblage was extensive and included a long rifle stored in a case shaped to indicate it was equipped with a scope. There was a shotgun and another rifle with a scope; a Colt short-stocked assault-type rifle, similar to an AR-15; another assault rifle similar to an AR-15 but cheaper, made from stamped metal. The collection also included a large plastic case, which apparently held handguns. From the size of the case, Sewell believed it held three to four guns. There was also a small zippered handgun case that held a small revolver.

Withholding this information had worried Sewell. He wanted to make certain that Dylhoff knew everything he knew about Russ and Khris Smith. He ended the conversation with one more piece of information.

"Russ revealed that sometime in mid-August he had done some work on a car he had purchased, then sold it. Russ said he had given Khris seventeen hundred dollars from the sale of the car, but he didn't know what she had done with the money. He said it was possible that she had stashed that money aside for her planned leaving," Sewell told the detective.

The money was news to Dylhoff. Why hadn't Smith told him about the cash when he asked about Khris's access to funds?

Tim and Debbie Orosz, the Smiths' neighbors directly to the north, took a special interest in the case and kept Dylhoff advised of any information provided them by Smith. The Oroszes had been close to the couple next door, and the abruptness of the Smiths' withdrawal from them had left unanswered questions in their minds.

Debbie Orosz had begun watching Lisa after school while Russ Smith was still at work. On the evening Tim Orosz contacted Dylhoff, Smith had come over to pick up his daughter and repeated the story of Khris's infidelity.

"I asked him why they had cut their friendship off from us. He indicated it was basically Khris's decision. He apologized for rudely cutting us off. Russ mentioned that every time they moved, Khris would do the same thing with relationships with neighbors. Then he told us he had dropped papers off at the school earlier in the day so that Khris wouldn't be able to pick Lisa up at school," Tim told him.

Dylhoff continued to make contact with those close to Khris Smith. He learned that in late August and early September Khris shared with friends her marital discontent. She never mentioned abuse. Never talked of leaving. She did speak of pursuing a new career. The avid outdoor enthusiast had mentioned landscaping as a possibility.

Friends described Khris Smith as a fun-loving flirt, at times going beyond innocence. Her flirting had even caused some discomfort, even embarrassment, among her friends.

Not one of Khris's acquaintances had heard from her. No one had any idea where she could have gone, or with whom.

Over the course of the next few weeks, bank records and credit card activity were rechecked—anything that would indicate Khris's location. But Smith had removed his wife's name from all banking records as well as all credit cards. If Khris Smith attempted to access funds, they would never know.

Both the All Star Cab Company and Rapid/Yellow Cab were contacted to find out if Khris had called for transportation on the day of her disappearance. Her car still remained in front of the Smith house.

The dentist Russ Smith claimed had treated Khris was no help in locating dental records. Khris had seen him only once, for an emergency visit. He had no dental records available. But through a system of calling one former dentist after another, anyone who had at any time seen Khris Smith, Dylhoff was finally able to locate a full set of dental X rays.

Charlene Lemons contacted Detective Dylhoff in an attempt to find out if anything new had developed in the investigation. She told Dylhoff that Lisa had been over several times in the past weeks and, in fact, had gone trick-or-treating with her children.

"When Russ dropped Lisa off, he stated, 'It's been a month today and I'm feeling very lonely,'" Charlene reported. Smith's shoulders drooped and the handsome smile Charlene remembered had vanished. "He also called a couple of times throughout the night, checking on Lisa to see how things were going."

According to Charlene, when asked by the Lemons children where Khris was, Lisa first stated her mother was at home; later, she told them she didn't actually know where her mother was and that she didn't want to talk about it. The seven-year-old's pain was obvious in her eyes.

It was strange to think that Khris Smith hadn't contacted her daughter on Halloween. Khris had always been very involved in the celebration and festivities of the October holiday. It was one of her favorite times of the year. She had always made certain that Lisa had a wonderful Halloween experience. It was out of character for Khris to ignore the fall merriment.

Dylhoff decided to contact the general manager of the Sears store in Lima, Ohio. Kurt Piska told the persistent detective that about a week after Khris left, Russ came down to Lima to talk.

When Piska asked his old friend if the police were looking at him for having something to do with his wife's disappearance, Smith said, "Yes, they are. But what do you tell them when you don't know anything? I don't know where Khris is."

As with so many people that Dylhoff had interviewed over the past month, the Lima Sears manager told of Smith's relating stories of Khris's infidelity. He stated that some of the stories Smith told him were real "gut wrenchers." He'd known Khris and Russ had problems before, but he thought it had all been worked out. This time he could feel the real pain his friend was dealing with.

After speaking with the Sears manager, Dylhoff walked to the evidence room of the Portage PD. He sifted through items recovered from the Smith garbage bin. Locating a piece of paper with $159.99 scrawled across it, along with a Portage address, Dylhoff decided to check it out.

The address was that of Kevin Canney. Canney had run an ad in the local newspaper to sell some of his guns and sporting equipment. Russ Smith had responded to the ad.

Smith had arrived at the Canney house in a silver-colored Dodge Dakota pickup truck. He'd looked at the guns Canney was selling, stating he was interested in an Interarms .44 magnum stainless-steel handgun with a nine-inch barrel. He'd also looked at a Mossberg shotgun. Canney wanted $300 for the two, but Smith countered with a cash offer of $250. Canney remembered Smith becoming angry when he refused the bid.

"This guy was really weird," Canney told Dylhoff. "I have a family member who is manic-depressive and this guy gave off the same vibes that my family member gives when I'm around him."

Dylhoff was interested to learn that Smith's contact

with Canney, and his perusal of the guns Canney had for sale, happened the day before Khris Smith disappeared.

Coincidence? Or a plan set in motion?

Chapter 7

At 9:00 P.M. on November 14, 1994, Russ Smith parked in the parking lot of the Portage City Complex and walked to the entrance of the Portage Police Department. Since it was after hours, he was forced to press the outside button to alert the dispatcher. Talking through the speaker mounted on the wall to the right of the secured front door, Russ Smith announced his appointment with Detective Randy Dylhoff and was buzzed through.

Passing a rack of information booklets, including a prominently placed pamphlet on domestic violence, and the window to the dispatcher's office, the white miniblind closed for the evening, Smith entered Dylhoff's office.

The interview was conducted at the Portage Police Department Annex, adjacent to the building that housed the detective's office. The interview room was bleak, free of decoration, and equipped with only a table and two chairs.

Dylhoff had asked Smith to bring the original copy of his wife's letter, but he didn't have it with him, saying that perhaps he had left the letter at his parents' house in Ohio.

Up until this point in the investigation, Russ Smith had been cooperative, even friendly toward Dylhoff.

When he arrived at the interview room, he appeared very defensive toward the detective.

"Can we again go over the events several days before Khris left and what occurred the day she left?" Dylhoff asked.

"I have a couple of questions myself," Smith retorted, laying out a letter from the Kalamazoo Credit Bureau on the table between himself and Dylhoff. Smith's face was stern, his jaw tight. The letter to the credit bureau had requested a copy of Smith's credit history.

"Why was this information needed?" Smith demanded.

Dylhoff attempted to explain that the Portage PD was conducting a credit check to determine what businesses they banked with and to determine if Khris was active on any accounts involving their credit.

"Will you go over the events the day Khris came up missing?" Dylhoff asked again, moving the conversation back to his purpose for the meeting.

"I've already told you those events," Smith snapped.

With Smith reluctantly cooperating, Dylhoff questioned him about the barrel of clothes and the additional items put in the back of his truck, about his trip to Ohio and then Florida, and his activities the day he learned Khris had left Portage.

Smith informed the detective that he took some of his wife's clothing to Déjà Vu, a strip club in Portage. The clothing, consisting of mostly high-heeled and spike-heeled shoes and some rather provocative clothing, was dropped off at the club for the girls who danced there.

"It was stuff Khris never wore for me," Smith said bitterly.

"How do you think Khris was going to get to Florida without a vehicle?" Dylhoff asked.

"I assumed her friend. Or maybe by plane or bus," Smith replied almost sarcastically.

Once again Smith reported his missing wife hadn't taken her keys to the house or her car when she left. He stated again that he'd found her wedding ring, which had been cut off, only upon his return.

Repeating his earlier statement, Smith said he had called home several times on his trip from his parents' home in Ohio as he headed to Florida, where Khris's mother lived. He reiterated that in response to one call home Khris had picked up the phone and hung up on him.

"How did you know it was Khris?" Dylhoff asked.

"She picked up the phone. It had to be her," Smith replied.

"Did she say hello, or did she just hang up?" Dylhoff inquired.

"I don't recall," Smith said.

Smith claimed he drove straight from Kentucky to his house in Portage, where he found his wife's ring when he entered the house. He insisted his wife left no note, other than the three-page letter she had given him before she left.

"Why did you advise me that Khris handed you the letter and you told other officers that she had left the letter behind and you found it?" Dylhoff asked.

"I don't know. The others must have misunderstood what I said, because she definitely handed me the letter," Smith said defensively. He appeared nervous, squirming in his chair, defensive in his answers.

Dylhoff wanted Smith's explanation for why he had told his mother-in-law that he and Khris had a terrible

fight and yet told Dylhoff there was only a verbal confrontation. Smith again insisted he and Khris had only
argued on the day she disappeared and he left the
house.

"And why did you tell her brother, Troy, that the
two of you had fought in the car several years ago,
with Khris spitting in your face?" Dylhoff probed.

"I just wanted people to be aware of what was going
on, and that this wasn't the first time she had done
something like this to me," Smith said with bitterness.

During the conversation Smith denied destroy-
ing any photos of Khris, other than pictures of the
two of them in what he described as "explicit" photos. "I didn't destroy anything that you would find
in a family photo album," Smith stated.

When Dylhoff questioned Smith whether he had
ever damaged any property in the past when he and
Khris had argued, or if any property had been damaged during their last dispute, Smith told the
detective about one incident, when he had thrown
a phone through the wall. The former reserve officer insisted there had been no major or minor
repairs to his kitchen or bathroom as a result of the
disagreement with his wife the day she left him.

Dylhoff leaned back in his straight-back chair and
studied Smith. Friends had reported Smith had in-
stalled a new tub and shower stall after Khris left for
parts unknown, yet Smith now denied causing any
damage to his house. Was Smith playing word
games? Or was he over his head and treading water
in an attempt to survive?

"I'm thinking about sending Lisa to her grandmother's in Florida for a while over Thanksgiving and
Christmas," Smith said, interrupting the questioning.

"But I'm concerned that, if I do, Khris might be there and take Lisa from me. I think Khris might be down in that area and nobody's telling me."

"I've talked to Kay and I know she has been quite upset and emotional over the whole deal," Dylhoff stated.

"Is this investigation starting to focus on me?" Smith asked bluntly.

"Where else are we to look at this point?" Dylhoff asked. The detective explained that Smith had been the last person to see Khris alive, and if he looked at the whole picture of what was going on, it did look suspicious.

"I think this interview has been 'let's shake the tree and see what falls,'" Smith said, referring to himself.

"There's one sure way to clear this up," Dylhoff replied, leaning forward toward Smith. "Take a polygraph."

Dylhoff explained to his suspect that, although a polygraph couldn't be used against Smith in a court of law, the county prosecutor relied on them heavily for eliminating people from suspicion.

"I've taken a couple of employment polygraphs in the past, but I'd have to consult with my attorney before I agreed to that," Smith said defensively.

With Smith agreeing to talk with his lawyer the following day, Smith was excused from the interview.

As Dylhoff watched his primary suspect pull out of the parking lot, he played the interview over in his head. The one thing that stuck out prominently was Russ Smith's anger toward his wife.

As Dylhoff expected, the following day Smith's attorney advised him that his client would not be taking the polygraph.

* * *

Dylhoff drove to Déjà Vu, the club where Smith claimed to have taken some of his wife's clothes. The gentle policeman was familiar with the club by reputation only. Dylhoff was a family man with a wife and two children he loved and adored. Unlike the men who kept the seedier Portage establishments thriving, Dylhoff only visited them on official police business.

In speaking to the strippers at the club, Dylhoff learned that Smith had brought several boxes of clothing items for them. They contained more than one hundred pairs of high-heeled, spike-type shoes. In addition, there were several pairs of pants, some dresses, and a half-dozen tank tops. The girls told Dylhoff that most of the clothing was very revealing, even suggestive. The dancers had even wondered if Smith's wife had once been a dancer herself, since the types of apparel he dropped off were like those usually worn by dancers.

"Why are you bringing these to us?" one of the strippers had asked.

"My wife doesn't want me anymore, so I'm donating these things to you girls," Smith had replied.

Dylhoff would later learn that Smith had apparently used his wife's clothing as an intro into the club—and to the strippers.

Dylhoff checked his prepared list of people to interview concerning the Khris Smith disappearance. He next headed to Lisa Smith's school.

Sue Warren was Lisa Smith's first-grade teacher at Angling Road Elementary School. She reported that Lisa was a good student and well liked by her classmates.

"Mr. Smith came to my class about noon that Wednesday and talked about taking Lisa out of school for a week, as well as the following Thursday and Friday," Warren informed Dylhoff. "I asked him why, and if there was a problem. I thought perhaps I could help in some way. He stated that there was a family emergency."

Warren described Smith as appearing very stressed and upset. He seemed to have difficulty talking about the breakup. Warren added that Smith had said that his wife left him that morning. He wanted Warren to get Lisa's work together for her so she wouldn't get too far behind.

"He didn't take her out of class early that day, but picked her up after school. When they got back, he gave me his business card and stated he was afraid Khris would come and get Lisa from school. He asked me if I would call him if Khris showed up. He also mentioned, a number of times, that Lisa was in counseling," Warren stated.

Exactly one month to the day that Khris Smith disappeared, Kay Klein and her son, Troy, called Detective Dylhoff.

"I just got back from Ohio," Kay stated. "I didn't like Russ's behavior during the time I was with him. When he called me on September twenty-eighth, his voice was very broken and distressed. Now Russ is acting differently. I feel he is just keeping me pacified."

Kay was very concerned with her granddaughter's behavior as well. Lisa told Kay, "If Mommy shows up, I'm going to call 911." Kay was convinced that Russ was brainwashing Lisa against her mother—something that Kay found incomprehensible considering the close relationship she knew her daughter and granddaughter shared.

"I believe Russ did something to Khris," Kay announced. "He wouldn't leave Lisa alone with me, except for two hours at the end of the weekend visit."

Smith had also advised Kay not to let Lisa go with Khris if she came by while he was gone. "He said he believed I knew more than I was telling him about Khris's whereabouts. He was very angry. But I asked him if he really thought I would withhold something from him or from the police. At that point Russ backed down and told me he hadn't meant to upset me."

Dylhoff could tell Kay Klein was getting worked up over Russ, but not until Troy joined the conversation did he realize her wrath was also directed toward him.

"We feel nothing is being done," Troy said sharply. "Why hasn't the FBI been involved in the investigation?"

Dylhoff put it as clearly as possible to Kay and Troy that the Portage PD was doing everything that could be done to find Khris. He advised them both that unless there was a crime committed that involved interstate flight, the FBI would not be involved.

Then Kay and Troy expressed their anger and frustration at not having received a copy of the police report, after making a request at least three weeks prior. Dylhoff tried to calm them and suggested that they contact the records division of the police department to learn why they hadn't received their requested copy.

Before hanging up with the Kleins, Dylhoff asked Kay if Khris had ever sought help from a psychiatrist, information Dylhoff had received when he contacted her general physician for the missing woman's health records.

"I remember when Lisa was nine months old, I went to visit for the first time. Khris made the comment to me, 'Mom, you have damaged me.' That was the only indication I had that Khris might have had some psychological problems."

Dylhoff barely had time to digest the information the Kleins had provided when his phone rang again. It was Troy Klein, without his mother.

"I contacted the FBI in Florida and you are correct. Unless there is some type of interstate flight involved, they won't join the investigation," Troy stated.

Dylhoff shook his head. Why couldn't some people accept the truth of what the police told them?

"They do have forensic and investigatory services available upon your agency's request. And they have psychological profiling services available that could work with Russ. He would have no idea that he was being interviewed as a suspect," Troy said, an edge of excitement in his voice.

"We would have to have the cooperation of the suspect," Dylhoff advised. "And at this point Russ has retained an attorney." Dylhoff knew there was no way Russ Smith's attorney was going to allow him to be interviewed by himself, much less observed by the FBI.

After considering his conversation with Troy Klein, Dylhoff dropped a copy of his report off at the local FBI office the following day for their information and possible input. The agent-in-charge advised him that he would review it, then forward it to their headquarters in Quantico, where it would be evaluated by their behavioral analysis unit (BAU).

Dylhoff felt confident that the FBI behavioral analyst would support his own gut feeling and streetwise deductions that Russ Smith was the person responsible for his wife's mysterious disappearance. But the fact remained, he was no closer to knowing what had happened the morning of September 28 than he had been a month earlier.

Chapter 8

Standing in their house on Thunderbay, Terry and Janet Pike looked out the window at the neighborhood. It was a normal, quiet Sunday afternoon. Kids played. Neighbors walked their dogs. The Pikes hadn't heard about the sudden and mysterious disappearance of their neighbor Khris Smith. They were somewhat alarmed as they observed a police officer walking around the Smith house, looking in the windows.

Terry Pike strolled across the street and began talking with Officer May Agay. He was surprised to hear of the mysterious departure of his neighbor. It was the first indication that he had that Khris Smith was no longer residing in the house. Neither Terry, an area schoolteacher, nor his wife, Janet, a part-time student and bank employee, had seen anything or heard anything concerning Khris Smith's leaving. Both Terry and Janet were gone during the day and seldom took notice of the daytime activities of the neighborhood.

Terry and Janet spoke with Detective Dylhoff a few days after learning of Khris's disappearance.

"The day after I spoke with Officer Agay, October third, Russ Smith stopped by our house about nine P.M.," Terry Pike said. "Russ said he knew there would be a lot of rumors going around the neighborhood.

He then asked us to read the letter Khris left and handed us a multiple-page letter."

Pike gave details of his conversation with Smith. Smith had told him the couple had been married eight years, that Khris had had numerous affairs, and that on Christmas Eve a couple of years earlier, Khris had gone out for the evening and hadn't come back until the next morning.

"Russ indicated [that] when Khris broke off that extramarital relationship, she went and got a teddy, toothbrush, and makeup from the guy's house," Terry Pike continued.

It was interesting that Russ Smith felt compelled to tell everyone he knew, regardless of how slightly, that Khris had conducted a number of affairs. Either Smith was hurt very badly and was dealing with his pain by "bleeding" all over everyone, or he was attempting to cover his ass. It was possible he was setting the stage for believability. When people lie, and lie, and lie, they are keeping a secret, something they want no one else to know. They become a performer on a stage. To paraphrase Shakespeare, "methinks he protests too much." Was Russ Smith lying?

Russ Smith told Pike and his wife about the argument on September 28, explaining that he had finally reached his breaking point and told Khris to get out. Dylhoff thought it interesting that Smith had gone through the entire scenario of leaving Portage to find Khris, the calls back home, and the cut wedding ring found upon his return with people he wasn't particularly close to.

Janet Pike had asked Smith if he thought Khris hadn't taken her car because he had been the one who worked to buy it, or perhaps she didn't want to take anything that belonged to him, anything that he had purchased.

"Russ said, 'Yes, that could be why,'" Janet said.

Terry added that Smith had also commented that since Khris had taken off with another guy, she didn't need a car. Smith had made a point of telling them he had put several thousand miles on his own truck looking for his wife.

Janet Pike had had limited contact with Khris during the time they all lived on Thunderbay, but she knew Khris was an unhappy woman.

"I went out a couple of times with Khris and a couple of other female friends. Khris made the comment to me that she was not allowed to have time on her own to get away. She indicated that [that] evening was the first time since she was married that she was allowed to get out of the house, to get away from her regular duties and responsibilities," Janet reported.

"Once Khris talked to me and other neighbors about changing the bus stop location. It is currently in front of the Smith house and when the weather was bad, Khris would keep the garage door open. Khris was always out there with Lisa. She allowed the other kids to come into the garage while they waited for the bus. Khris wanted someone else to have that duty and responsibility this year," Janet stated, adding that perhaps Khris knew she would be leaving and wanted to make the bus stop change ahead of time.

Russ Smith had told the Pikes he believed Khris had been planning her exodus. She had made a detailed schedule of Lisa's various activity days, when she had to get up, and the places she had to go. Russ Smith seemed to believe Khris had left the schedule so he would know what to do.

* * *

Tim and Debbie Orosz were the kind of neighbors who always kept an eye on the neighborhood. They made themselves the "neighborhood watch," and after Khris Smith's disappearance, the Russ Smith watchdogs.

Debbie Orosz saw Lisa Smith nearly every day. The seven-year-old would come to the Orosz house frequently to play with the Orosz children. Debbie observed that the first month or so after Khris left, Lisa's schedule was less rigid and the time restraints seemed to have disappeared. Lisa appeared much more relaxed, but then her familiar paranoia about being home at five o'clock returned.

Tim Orosz, like his wife, Debbie, kept a watchful eye on Russ Smith's comings and goings and the activities around his house. On Sunday, November 27, 1994, Tim noticed Smith next door in his driveway, gutting out a deer.

"I went over to see what was going on," Tim told Dylhoff when they spoke a few days later. "Russ indicated he had just gotten back from his folks and the car in front of him had hit a deer. The people didn't want it, so Russ took it. Russ was asking questions about the proper way to gut the deer, which I thought was strange because Russ had gone hunting and killed deer before. He always talked like he was an avid hunter."

Tim added that Russ had hunted near the Mentha Drain area, northeast of Kalamazoo, near the Timber Ridge ski area. The out-of-the way area, on the way to Otsego and Plainwell, was a favorite hunting spot of a friend of Smith's who owned property in that vicinity.

Dylhoff was unclear as to why Tim Orosz mentioned

the hunting area or Smith's ability to field dress a deer. Perhaps he thought Khris's body might be found in the Mentha Drain area, but at that time there was no evidence that Khris Smith had met an untimely death, or that her husband would be found responsible.

Khris Smith's medical records indicated that Khris had seen her physician for vaginal and pelvic problems that included discomfort distinctly related to intercourse. According to the records, if Khris and Russ Smith abstained from intercourse, there was no problem; but each and every time she and her husband had sex, approximately six hours later, she had an onset of pelvic pain. An ultrasound had been performed. It revealed nothing.

Was Khris Smith's pain real or imagined? Was Khris displaying a subtle abuse of her husband by withholding sex under the pretense of physical pain? She may well have been displaying her contempt and rage at Russ by exhibiting passive-aggressive behavior.

The doctor's notes included a reference on August 1, 1994, that Khris complained that she got angry at the slightest things that didn't go her way. She stated that her anger had led to multiple conflicts at home with both her husband and her daughter. The doctor had referred Khris to Westside Mental Health for attention deficit disorder. He stated in his notes, "I certainly think this evaluation is in order, not for the ADD, but mainly for any counseling or help this family can get in dealing with each other better than they currently do."

Six weeks prior to Khris Smith's mysterious disappearance, her own physician had seen a family in turmoil, a family in need of immediate help. Records indicated that the Smiths never took the doctor's advice.

By this stage in the investigation, Detective Randy Dylhoff and suspect Russ Smith had developed a strangely pleasant rapport. Dylhoff believed that if he was going to get Smith to confess to knowing the whereabouts of his wife, it would be done by buddying up with Smith. Smith had already proven he would hide behind his lawyer if confronted head-on.

After the Thanksgiving holidays Dylhoff stopped by Smith's house to see how his weekend in Ohio had gone.

"It went well," Smith said. "I no longer believe Khris's family knows where she is. At first I was concerned about letting Lisa go with Kay, who was in Ohio visiting her mother. I was worried that Khris might be around and take Lisa, but the last day I let Kay have Lisa for an hour or so by herself."

Smith denied having any type of correspondence with Khris or anyone who might know where she was. There still had been no activity by Khris on their bank accounts. Russ had added, almost as an afterthought, "I have been getting some hang-up calls from out of the area that have shown up on my caller ID."

"If you're concerned we can put a trace on the phone and locate where the calls are coming from," Dylhoff suggested.

Smith declined, stating that the calls mainly came during the day when he wasn't at home. "They usually occur around four P.M. after Lisa gets home. If I'm home and pick up the phone, there is silence and then the person hangs up. If it's Khris, she might be anticipating Lisa answering the phone."

"One way to find out if it's Khris is to let Lisa answer the phone," Dylhoff recommended.

Smith ignored the detective's proposal, explaining that Lisa had been outside when he answered the one hang-up call.

"In contacting some of the neighbors, they indicated something about a blue-colored boat in your yard the same week that Khris came up missing. Do you recall whose boat that was?" Dylhoff asked.

Smith couldn't seem to call to mind any boat meeting the description Dylhoff gave. Smith also denied that Khris had been to a psychologist, had any physical health problems, or took any prescribed medications.

Before leaving, Dylhoff informed Smith, "We'll be running an article, along with a photo of Khris, in the newspaper."

Russ Smith had given the detective the most recent photo he had of his wife during an earlier visit. He went to the photo album, which rested on the living-room table and extracted an eight-by-ten picture of Khris when her hair was long and blond.

Dylhoff studied the photo with great interest. He couldn't believe it was Khris Smith. No one would ever recognize her. Her hair had been lightened considerably, but the dark roots gave her away as a natural brunette.

"Lisa wanted her hair changed last week, so I got a hair color kit and did it myself," Smith said. He chuckled as he explained to Dylhoff that Lisa's hair had turned burned orange and he had ended up taking his seven-year-old daughter to a professional salon for a color treatment. Lisa's beautiful sandy-blonde locks had been converted to a shade somewhere between a light reddish brown and a strawberry blond. Lisa now looked more like her missing mother—the woman Smith told his mother-in-law he missed terribly. The veteran cop stared at Smith with concern.

"Do you mind if I talk to Lisa alone?" Dylhoff asked.

"I would prefer that you don't," Smith replied.

"Well, I just wanted to let you know we're running the article and photo in the paper," Dylhoff said, then slyly added, "After it comes out, I don't know what type of inquiries there will be. Would you like to try and clear things up before the article runs?"

Smith declined, again stating that he would not say any more without consulting his attorney. He specifically stated that he was going to exercise his rights and stick with the recommendation of his attorney.

Dylhoff knew it was going to take more time to get Smith to trust him enough to tell him what really happened on the morning of September 28, 1994.

The Khris Smith investigation hadn't reaped sufficient evidence to indict Russ Smith for the murder of his wife. Just as the book *Corpus Delicti,* on Russ Smith's living-room table, said: "You only have to prove, even in a circumstantial evidence case, two elements: first, that death occurred, and second, by some criminal means." At this point in the investigation, neither element could be confirmed. Nonetheless, Dylhoff wanted the assistant prosecutor to take a look at it, perhaps to give direction as to which way the investigation should go.

The assistant prosecuting attorney Bob Pangle agreed with the detective; there were a number of unusual circumstances. However, he also agreed that at this point they would be unable to prove that a crime had even occurred. He was hesitant to review the case fully, to look at it from an investigative angle due to liability issues. Pangle advised Dylhoff that if they came up with something solid, or if they needed a search warrant, he would be more than willing to have someone from his office review the investigative file and discuss it at that time.

Dylhoff's conversation with the assistant prosecutor went just as he had expected. He knew he had more work to do before proving both elements of the crime: to prove that a death had occurred and that Russ Smith was the killer.

Chapter 9

Lisa Smith attended school, played with her friends, and went to dance lessons—just as she had done before her mother vanished.

To the shock and amazement of her teacher and classmates, in mid-December Lisa showed up at school with her hair colored. When Sue Warren asked her student what she had done with her hair, Lisa had responded, "My dad wanted to know if I wanted to dye it, so he did. He dyed it at home and it turned orange, so we then had to go to a beauty parlor to get it to the color that it is now."

Later that week, Russ Smith went to the school to talk with Sue Warren. "What do you think of Lisa's hair?" Smith had asked, obviously pleased with his child's new look. "She's been bugging and teasing me to lighten her hair. I didn't think that it would be that hard, so we did it at home. It turned orange. Then I had to take her to a beauty parlor, where they got it to the strawberry blond, which it is now."

Smith had taken his daughter to a professional hairdresser to straighten out the mess he made of Lisa's hair. The cosmetologist had been working in the beauty field for 2½ years, but she had never colored the hair of a child as young as Lisa Smith, or seen it done.

Warren was concerned because the comments

made by Russ and Lisa Smith differed in whose idea it was to color a seven-year-old's hair. She decided to ask Lisa for further illumination.

"Your daddy told me you'd been teasing and bugging him to have your hair dyed," Warren began.

"No, he asked me if I wanted it dyed," Lisa corrected the teacher.

"Did you go to the store and buy the color?" Warren asked.

"No, it was some stuff that we had at home," Lisa replied.

Sue Warren was concerned for Lisa Smith. She was a likable, bright child who had been looking very tired the last few weeks. Lisa had told her that Monday nights were her "late nights" when she was at the day care until 10:00 P.M. Lisa said that after Christmas she'd be staying late on Friday nights, rather than a school night. Warren hoped that would help the child, but she was certain the problem was much deeper than a late night at day care.

In talking with a fellow teacher about her concerns for Lisa, Warren learned that Lisa had told the teacher she wanted a new mother for Christmas.

Sue Warren called Detective Dylhoff and related the conversations and her concerns.

The Portage Police Department again checked with Khris Smith's prescription card network to see if she had renewed her prescription for acne cream. They learned there had been no activity on the card since before September 28.

Phone contact was made with the Florida Department of Law Enforcement (FDLE) concerning the

Michigan Law Enforcement Bulletin containing information about Khris Smith's disappearance. Inez Peterson agreed to run an article in their state publication that would be seen by all Florida law enforcement agencies and some federal agencies in that area.

The Portage Police Department was leaving no stone unturned in their investigation of Khris Smith's missing status. Their inquiries included the Cridersville, Ohio, Police Department, where Russ Smith had once worked. They learned he had applied with the Cridersville Police Department on March 3, 1984, and took the oath of office on April 2, 1984. He immediately began work as an auxiliary officer working a minimum of sixteen hours per month. The record showed Smith worked many more hours above the minimum required.

On April 27, 1990, Russ Smith resigned his commission as a Cridersville police officer. His letter of resignation stated he was being transferred by Sears, his full-time employer, to another location.

Investigators knew that Russ Smith met Khris Klein while working for both Sears and the Cridersville PD.

Detectives Dylhoff and Romanak went to Khris Smith's grandmother's house in Elida, Ohio. Although no one was there, a close neighbor informed the detectives that she hadn't seen Khris Smith or anyone meeting her description near the residence in recent weeks. She promised to notify them if Khris showed up there.

Next the investigative duo traveled to Lima, Ohio, and the neighborhood where the Smiths once lived. Carol Linser, who had lived across the street from Russ and Khris, stated she hadn't known them well but was familiar with the couple.

Linser had heard rumors about Khris Smith messing around and having different affairs, but she had
no firsthand information if the stories were fact or
neighborhood gossip.

"At times they seemed to have a good marriage,
and at other times it was strange because Khris would
wear really tight jeans and skimpy outfits," Linser told
Dylhoff and Romanak. The former neighbor seemed
to be implying Khris Smith's wardrobe reflected the
mood of her marriage.

From Lima, Dylhoff and Romanak traveled less
than twenty miles south to Cridersville. The first snow
of the season had already begun to fall and a thin coat
of white dusted the trees along the route. The small
town of approximately eighteen hundred people was
the boyhood home of Russ Smith and the continual
residence of his parents.

After answering the knock on her door, Linda
Smith stepped outside, closing the door of her home
behind her. Lisa and another of the Smiths' grand-
children remained inside, behind the closed door.

Dylhoff explained that he and Detective Romanak
were there to investigate the disappearance of Khris
Smith. With her back against her front door, the elder
Mrs. Smith stated she had heard nothing other than
the fact that Khris had left her son.

"I received a phone call from Russ. He stated, 'She
has left me.' I asked him, 'Who? Khris?' He said, 'Yes,'"
Linda Smith reported as frosty air escaped her mouth.

Russ Smith had told his mother the same story he'd
related to everyone the detectives had talked to. He
believed Khris was going to Florida to her mom's.

Russ had dropped Lisa off at his mother's in the early
evening, along with the rabbit, the cage, and Lisa's bike.

Linda Smith didn't recall seeing anything else in the back of her son's truck, although she hadn't gone outside while he unloaded the bike and cage.

Although Smith's mother had requested he call her periodically from along the road, she didn't get the first call until about seven o'clock the next morning. During that call he informed his mother that he thought Khris was home because someone had picked up the phone during one of his calls. He'd told her he was headed back to Portage. Linda didn't receive another phone call until Smith was back in his house. He told his mother he had found the garage-door opener and Khris's wedding ring set, which had been cut off, in the house.

According to his mother, Russ Smith didn't return to Cridersville for two to four days to pick up his daughter. Mrs. Smith was not in possession of the letter Khris had left her husband or her daughter-in-law's wedding rings, as Smith had informed Dylhoff.

Linda Smith thought Khris a rather strange person. She voiced no surprise that her daughter-in-law would just up and leave her son. Linda complained that Khris had made no effort to get close to any of her in-laws, even though Linda had tried to get close to Khris. As Russ Smith had done earlier, Linda related the story of the family wedding that Khris refused to be a part of.

Smith's mother was unaware of any affair or liaisons her daughter-in-law may have had, claiming she and Russ never spoke of such things. "I don't get involved with my children's relationships or how they raise their children," Linda stated.

But Linda did comment on a strange thing that Khris did when Lisa was four years old.

"She bleached Lisa's hair white. When we went to Lisa's dance recital, I didn't even recognize my own granddaughter. I couldn't believe what Khris had done. I didn't ask about it or say anything about it," Linda remarked as she ran her fingers through her own naturally white hair.

"I also thought Khris had Lisa doing too many things. She was in piano lessons, dance lessons, T-ball, and various other activities. It seemed like Khris was reliving her life through Lisa. But I said nothing. Khris was a good mother and did care for Lisa," Linda stated.

Still standing on the porch of the Smith home with the cold December air biting at their exposed faces, Dylhoff and Romanak asked if Khris had been the cause of the breakup of Russ's first marriage, to Lucia. If Linda Smith knew the answer, she wasn't telling. Linda did claim she and her husband were good friends with Lucia's parents and frequently went north to Lake Erie together.

The initially defensive and reluctant Mrs. Smith had been cordial and helpful. She assured the detectives she would have no problem talking with them again if they needed any further information or if other things developed.

Lucia Smith was next on the long list of people to interview. Smith's former wife was living in Lima, Ohio, and although she had retained the last name of Smith, she often went by Guisinger, the name of her common-law husband.

Russ and Lucia Smith had been married on June 23, 1984, and divorced in April 1986. The couple had basically grown up together, gone to school together, and their parents remained good friends. Through-

out their marriage Russ had never physically abused
Lucia, but he did have a temper. While installing a
ceiling fan in their first house, Russ and Lucia had
gotten into a bit of an argument and Russ had put his
fist through a wall. The angry gesture had made him
mad at himself, knowing he would have to repair the
wall to make it right.

According to Lucia, her ex-husband had been sexually demanding during their marriage. "Russ wanted
sex every night and I wouldn't put up with that,"
Lucia said. "After a couple of nights of no sex, he
would want it from me and I would tell him no. Then
he would back off and pout."

Toward the end of their relationship, Smith accused his wife of "messing around" with four of his
friends from the Cridersville Police Department.
Smith would even follow her when she went out. Yet,
it hadn't been Lucia who had been seeing others outside the marriage, but Smith himself.

"When I came home from work one night, Russ was
sitting in the house. The television was gone, along
with a few other things. He told me he wanted out. We
talked for several hours, but nothing was resolved. He
moved out; then within two weeks I found out I was
pregnant. Russ moved back in, but when I lost the
baby, he moved out again. He had shown no desire to
have children. He was preoccupied with car shows
and police work," Lucia reported.

Lucia stated that although many of Smith's friends
thought the promotions he had gotten at his job had
gone to his head, causing him to act uppity and too
good to associate with the people in Cridersville, she
and Russ had remained friends after the divorce. In
fact, after Smith married Khris and she was expecting

their child, Russ Smith had gone to Lucia's house, indicating he wanted to get back together with her. Lucia advised him he had already made his choice and that there was no way they were getting back together.

As with many in the small town, Lucia had heard Khris "got around" with the males in the community, but she didn't feel Russ Smith was the type to hurt anyone.

Kelly Gardner was not so certain. She had lived next door to the Smiths in Lima, Ohio. Although she claimed not to know Smith well, she thought he was strange. He wasn't the talkative sort, he didn't get along well with other males in the neighborhood, and then there was the time Smith was on his roof with a gun.

Gardner had feared Smith was going to shoot her dog. Smith assured her he had no intention of harming the animal; he was up there to shoot birds. It frightened Gardner. Every time she saw Smith, he had a gun with him. Although he was only a reserve officer on the Cridersville police force, he seemed to always be in uniform. The uniform and gun appeared to give Smith the sense of power and importance he otherwise lacked.

Gardner reported that Khris Smith, unlike her husband, was outgoing and vivacious. She had confided in Gardner that she was having an affair with a man who worked at the PicWay shoe store. Lisa was almost two years old at the time. Khris divulged that she had taken Lisa with her when she would meet the man at different motels in the area. She had even entertained him at the Smiths' home on Paradise Street in Lima. Gardner was certain Russ Smith was unaware of the affair.

Khris worked nights at the Holiday Inn bar. Her

uniform consisted of tights and a skimpy, alluring costume. Smith disapproved of his wife's job, but Khris ignored his objections and continued working at the bar until two or three o'clock each morning.

Khris's propensity for provocative, eye-catching clothing was not limited to her employment. Gardner mentioned that when the trim on the Smiths' Lima house needed painting, Khris was seen painting in a bikini and peach-colored high-heeled shoes. Her behavior screamed that she craved attention from men. And she got it.

When a new house was being constructed down the street from her Paradise Street home, Khris often stopped by to visit with the workmen. She would be wearing a very short, tight jeans skirt and a tank top, or some similar sexually revealing outfit. Khris had a good figure and liked to show it off. She seemed to thrive on the attention of men.

Lisa was breast-fed until she was four years old. Perhaps because Khris liked the fullness of her breasts, or maybe she wanted to be seen with her breasts publicly exposed. Gardner stated she often observed Khris sitting in her car nursing Lisa. Khris's explanation was that whenever they got into the car, Lisa would want to nurse, a justification Gardner thought outlandish.

Perhaps her body was all Khris felt she had control of. Russ Smith regulated the remainder of her life, including the family finances. According to Gardner, Smith was very tight with his money, often yelling at Khris for buying a dress or some other article that he deemed unnecessary.

Russ Smith also appeared to dominate their sex life. Khris had confided in Gardner that her husband wanted sex much more often than she did. She

indicated that at times Russ would even force himself upon her when she didn't really want to have
sex.

Gardner was not surprised to hear Khris had left
her husband, since Gardner viewed Russ Smith as a
sneaky, meek-type person who was periodically un-
truthful. She saw Khris Smith as a woman who had
some deep emotional problems.

Kelly Gardner believed the Smiths were a potentially
combustible combination.

Chapter 10

Russ Smith was beginning a metamorphosis, changing his look and his personality. Tim and Debbie Orosz noticed the change as they kept a vigil on their neighbor's comings and goings and the people who frequented the Smith house. They were surprised to see Smith pull into his driveway in a shiny red car instead of his familiar older model pickup truck. But when Smith began bringing women to the house less than three months after his wife's disappearance, Tim and Debbie were flabbergasted, and appalled.

Don Sewell, Smith's boss, noticed Smith's transformation with amazement and disbelief.

Russ Smith had advised his boss he was looking at a 1994 GT Mustang and wondered if Sewell had ever driven one. The two men went out to the local Ford dealership, taking one of the new model Mustangs for a spin. Smith ended up buying the cherry red sports car, using his pickup as a trade-in. The flashy car seemed fitting for Smith's new persona.

In conjunction with his newly assumed character traits, Smith's ambition was at an all-time high. Smith had been passed up for a couple of promotions at Sears, and Smith had questioned his boss about the oversight. He learned that the store, as a whole, was concerned about Smith's family situation. Sears didn't want to create any additional stress or problems for Smith than he was already having to handle, especially since the company was trying to make the adjustment to Smith's new status as a single parent.

"Russ told me that if he had a shot at a promotional position, he would be able to take Lisa down to his parents and she could live with them for a while," Sewell informed Dylhoff when the detective recontacted Smith's boss.

Smith certainly appeared to be ambitious. He was willing to sacrifice time with his daughter in order to move up in the company.

Dylhoff questioned Sewell about a fishing trip on Atwater Pond that Sewell and Smith had taken. Smith had caught a largemouth bass. He'd had it mounted and displayed prominently in his home. Sewell informed the detective that he and Smith had rented a boat from the boat launch at the pond, since neither man owned a boat at the time.

Dylhoff had also questioned Sewell in regard to the barrel reported to have been in Smith's truck the day his wife disappeared. He also asked him about the one he had seen in Smith's basement. Sewell was not familiar with the barrels, but he promised to look into them and get back with Dylhoff, which he did later in the week.

"I went down by the loading dock area and found one of the dark barrels that looked new, with a ring on the top as you described," Sewell reported. "That barrel has been there for two to three months and was left by a company that removes sludge from our drains. One of the employees advised that there are usually two to three of those on-site. I'll check with the sludge company and try to track down how many barrels were left and when."

According to Sewell, it would be difficult to know for certain if the barrel in Smith's garage and the one seen in the back of his pickup truck were taken from the Sears dock. As Sears Auto Center manager, Smith was responsible for ordering the barrels. It would have been possible for Smith to make some type of deal for barrels for his personal use, since he would have had access to the delivery companies and businesses that handled that type of item. Sewell declared that if anything further was needed, Russ Smith would have to be confronted, something Sewell suggested he preferred not to do.

Dylhoff wasn't certain how the barrels fit into the disappearance of Khris Smith, but his usually reliable instinct told him there was some connection.

Russ Smith's new car, his less conservative clothing, and the earring he wore in his right ear were the outward expressions of a man who had burst out of his shy shell.

Sears employees reported that at the annual store Christmas party, Russ became somewhat intoxicated. He carried mistletoe from female to female, held it above their heads, and kissed them. The act was quite out of character for Smith, who was usually quiet and reserved and had normally positioned himself against a wall, far away from the holiday merriment. He had never before been seen intoxicated at any company function.

Smith had also begun tanning, more than likely using the tanning bed his missing wife had prized so much. He bragged about his new car and the expensive grandfather clock for his parents' Christmas present. He had taken Lisa to the beauty shop again to have her hair colored, this time to a golden blond. All these things were uncharacteristic of Russ Smith. No one at Sears understood the changes taking place in him. He seemingly had gone from introvert to extrovert, dull to flashy, in just over a month. Had the narcissistic personality always been hidden just below the surface? Had his wife's assertive personality overshadowed him through all those years of marriage? His friends were beginning to wonder: who was the real Russ Smith?

Along with Sewell, Rick Lemons was recontacted by Dylhoff in reference to detailed information concerning Lemons assisting Smith with a damaged water line.

Smith had stopped by the Lemonses' house on December 23, 1994, nearly two months after Khris left, to show off his new red Mustang. When Smith told Lemons he had traded in a vehicle, Lemons asked if he had traded in Khris's car.

"No," Smith replied. "I traded in my truck. I still have Khris's car. The car belongs to her. It's hers if she comes back."

Smith admitted to Lemons that the police had been to Ohio to talk with his parents, his brothers, and some friends in that area. Smith hadn't seemed too pleased with the detectives' probe into his possible involvement in Khris's disappearance.

"Russ called on October fourteenth to see if I could patch a pipe on his shower. Two days later, I stopped by Russ's house on my way home from work and patched the copper pipe for the water line. I work in refrigeration, so I had a special solder, which would mend small puncture holes.

"The hole was definitely a nail puncture and was on the outside wall of the main tub, four to five inches up off the floor. Russ apparently was pounding a nail through the fiberglass and missed the stud, hitting the pipe. That was the only open portion of the wall I saw. Russ had already replaced the drywall around the top of the tub. The replacement kit Russ put in was actually four pieces, a three-piece wall kit and the tub itself. I didn't notice any other patch marks or holes. The tub and shower was replaced in the upstairs hall bathroom. Not the bath off the master bedroom," Lemons told Dylhoff.

Lemons couldn't remember exactly why Smith said he had to replace the tub/shower unit, but it was something to do with his getting upset and punching a hole in the wall part of the enclosure. Lemons hadn't seen the old unit and didn't know what Smith had done with it.

Dylhoff had wanted to get his hands on the discarded tub/shower unit, believing many of his questions would be answered. How much damage had been done to the structure? And would there be any telltale traces of blood found on the surface? But Dylhoff knew those questions might never be answered.

Dylhoff hoped he would have better luck with Smith's traded truck. He contacted Seelye Ford, where Smith had purchased the Mustang and sold his truck. The vehicle was buried under a recent snowfall. It would be days before the detective could take a look at the pickup, with the hope of finding some sort of evidence linking Smith to his wife's disappearance.

Four days later, Dylhoff was informed that the truck had been sold and would be picked up that afternoon. Dylhoff's optimism sank. If the truck had been detailed for resale, evidence may have been washed away.

The manager of Seelye Ford's West Main Street location asked Dylhoff not to contact the new owner until the sale was complete. He feared the deal might be lost if the buyer learned the vehicle might hold evidence regarding a missing person where foul play was suspected.

Dylhoff shook his head in frustration.

When Dylhoff returned to his office after speaking with the used-car manager at Seelye, he found three pages of notes left by Lieutenant Sue Blodgett. Apparently, a female by the name of Michelle had contacted the department concerning Russ Smith.

The notes indicated that Michelle met Russ Smith shortly after Thanksgiving when she answered a personal ad Smith had placed in the local newspaper.

"QUIXOTIC"

I'm 32 years old, 6´1´´, 175 lbs. I enjoy most outdoor activities as well as quiet times at home. ISO attractive female for adventurous friendship. Kalamazoo area, code 3587.

Smith had told Michelle by phone that his wife had just left him and that he had had an inkling it would happen.

Michelle agreed to meet Smith at his home. Her note said, "His house has a woman's touch, and I couldn't believe she would walk away from it."

Michelle thought it strange that during her visit

Smith kept the lights off throughout the house except for the one in the family room. Even as he took her upstairs to show her his computer, he hadn't turned on any lights in the stairway or hall. He hadn't even turned on the light in the computer room. She also thought it strange that he hadn't offered to show her around the rest of his house.

Smith and Michelle had drunk wine and he talked about Lisa, who, he claimed, was upstairs asleep. Michelle wrote that Smith talked at length about having to keep up with his daughter's schedule. She never saw Lisa, not even a photo, since there were no pictures of anyone around the house.

Smith told Michelle he had filed for divorce but had to wait for the final decree, since his wife's whereabouts were unknown. He didn't talk about his problems, didn't say he was looking for Khris, and he never appeared concerned, Michelle had written. He also claimed his daughter never asked about her mother.

Michelle said she felt uncomfortable talking with Smith. It seemed his mouth was saying one thing and his body language another. She suspected he was not being honest with her and was hiding something. She termed him "secretive."

Michelle had friends in Smith's neighborhood who had a child Lisa's age. When asked if he knew them, Smith stated he didn't know any of his neighbors very well. He added that Lisa didn't go outside much. These statements only added to Michelle's sense that Russ Smith was a very peculiar man with secrets to hide.

Michelle, although claiming not to be into astrology, stated she kept a log of people she came into contact with, along with their dates of birth. After looking Smith's birth date up in one of her astrology books, she believed he would be very domineering and treat his wife like a peon. The potential for a spouse or lover to leave would be strong. She surmised he would be a difficult father and husband, although outwardly charming.

Although Smith had told Michelle he was looking for an intimate relationship, he made her uneasy, negating any sexual attraction.

Detectives Tom Palenick and Gwen Romanak, along with Sergeant Don Anderson, were added to the investigation once the case had been upgraded from a missing persons to a possible homicide. They discussed the Khris Smith case at length with Detective Dylhoff, going over all the information gathered to date. On January 10, 1995, Detective Palenick completed a seven-page search warrant affidavit. The following day, the warrant was signed by the Honorable Robert Kropf of the 9-2 District Court. Finally Portage police would have access to the house on Thunderbay where Khris Smith was last seen.

On January 11, 1995, the search warrant service team, consisting of Detectives Palenick, Dylhoff, Romanak, and Jess Kalis, as well as Sergeant Pat Kimble and Officer Paul Sherfiled, arrived at the Russ Smith residence. Smith was unexpectedly home early.

"We have a search warrant prepared for your residence," Palenick informed Smith.

Smith let the service team inside without any problems or questions. He stood silent as he was read his Miranda rights, only speaking to acknowledge he understood.

Detective Palenick personally read the search warrant and complete affidavit to Smith, in case he had any questions regarding the procedure. But Smith had none. Palenick found Smith's silence strange, since many of the points in the affidavit would have been unknown to Smith, including the fact that the missing person status of Khris Smith was now considered a death investigation, with Smith himself as the prime suspect. The detective's eyes narrowed as he studied Smith and the uncharacteristic response to being considered a suspect in his wife's disappearance.

Also referenced in the affidavit were a number of points that stated that Russ Smith had apparently lied to detectives. Smith's expression never changed when the allegations were read and he made no comment.

Lowering the affidavit and looking in the face of Russ Smith, Palenick asked, "Would you mind answering some questions?"

"I'm afraid I can't answer any questions. I'll be leaving for a hockey game in about twenty minutes. Can you get me a pair of pants and a belt from the upstairs bedroom?"

Smith's coolness and calm exterior puzzled the detectives. Was he just a coldhearted bastard? Or was he smug enough to believe he had gotten away with murder?

Smith changed his clothes, shook Palenick's hand, and told the detective to contact him on his pager if he needed anything. Then their prime suspect was gone for a night out.

The search warrant itself was fairly lengthy and included financial, medical, and phone records. The long search began.

A search of the residence revealed that there were no photographs on the walls, fireplace mantel, or anywhere else in the residence, just as Michelle's note had stated. The only photo found was in a frame on the headboard in the master bedroom. The picture was of Lisa Smith, standing by a large person in a teddy bear costume.

Except for a plastic pail in the basement, containing clothing belonging to Khris Smith and jewelry in a case in Lisa's bedroom, there were no other signs that the missing woman had ever resided at the home. Her personal touches remained, however.

In the dining room, the hunter green sidewall held pictures along with a wooden shelf containing a teapot, green plant, and a small wreath adorned with narrow ribbon. The window valance was floral. The brass vase on the table, holding a spray of green eucalyptus and red flowers, sat on a country-motif runner with fringed trim.

The kitchen walls were covered with a small purple-and-green-print wallpaper, accented with a border of large purple violets. A chintz valance hung over the kitchen window, where a potted plant sat on the ledge next to a small birdhouse. The kitchen, as in all other rooms of the house, had a definite female presence.

The search quickly concentrated on the upstairs bathroom, where Rick Lemons had helped Russ Smith repair a water line. The area had obviously been completely redone by Smith. New square tile flooring had been placed over the top of the original linoleum flooring. The walls sported fresh, new wallpaper in a vertical flower-striped design with matching border. The border hung precariously from the top of the wall, as if hung in haste. When the baseboard was removed, it was evident that new drywall had been hung as well.

The investigators looked one to the other. The

house had been completed as a new structure just after June 1992. That made the entire interior of the home, including the bathroom completely remodeled by Russ Smith, just over two years old. Without speaking, each investigator wondered if there was any reason for the sudden update other than Russ Smith's attempting to hide something.

The service team discussed removing the shower stall, along with the flooring. It was decided at that time they wouldn't take out the shower, but removal would remain a possibility for later scrutiny.

In searching through Smith's records, no accounts past August 1994 were available. Russ Smith apparently had gone through everything in the residence carefully and removed anything that would have a current record at or about the time that Khris Smith disappeared. There were no phone records found at all. No wonder Russ Smith had looked so smug at the time the warrant was served. He knew he had carefully removed most of the information the police were searching for. An additional search warrant would be completed to obtain the phone records for January 1 through December 31, 1994, from the telephone company. Warrants would also be drawn up for credit histories for both Russ and Khris Smith and for any additional information that might be needed.

During the extensive search of the Smith house, a photo album, the one Detective Dylhoff had noticed on a prior visit, was found. The photo collection contained pictures of all rooms in the interior of the residence. Dates and other handwritten information about the rooms appeared on the back of each photo. From the cursive writing, it was concluded that Khris

Smith had been the one who had kept the meticulous record of their Portage, Michigan, home.

The detectives studied the photo of the upstairs bathroom with interest. Russ Smith apparently had removed pictures of the original bathroom and replaced them with photos taken after the room had been remodeled. They were the only photos in the entire album that were not dated or in some way identified in the handwriting of Khris Smith. Russ Smith had clearly gone to elaborate means in an attempt to hide the reconstruction of the upstairs bath.

In going through the album, the detectives were able to find a negative with a different image of the interior of the bathroom, one they believed to have been taken prior to the remodeling. They would have prints made as soon as possible and a search warrant for further examination of the bath area would be drawn up.

As the search of Smith's home continued, numerous Sears items were found throughout the house. Some were brand-new. In the closet of the master bedroom, there were three mini camcorders, two of them the same model and brand. Two were located in a box on a shelf. Smith had apparently been using the third.

In the basement searchers found snowblowers, mag wheels, leafblowers, and a variety of other new Sears merchandise. Tim Orosz had told Detective Dylhoff that Smith had held frequent garage sales and had mentioned a number of Sears items that had been for sale. Dylhoff made a mental note to check with Sears concerning the merchandise found in the Smith home.

Seven maps of various states, along with a number of city maps, were found in Smith's house. Written on a Pensacola, Florida, map were Baroco-Rogers Realty and Re-Max Horizon Realty, along with each agency's address and phone number. Dylhoff asked himself if Smith had plans to relocate. And how quickly?

The investigation was gaining momentum. The search team could feel the case coming together. With each discovery they became more exhilarated, more certain they were on the right track, *and* after the right suspect.

But the feelings of anticipation and satisfaction were short-lived. Lisa Smith's room was thoroughly probed, as was Russ Smith's master bedroom, during the search. All of seven-year-old Lisa's clothes were hanging on one side of her father's closet. It appeared they had been placed where her mother's clothing had previously hung. All of Lisa's underclothing had been moved from her room to Smith's bedroom dresser. A flannel sleeper, which zipped up the front and had legs with feet, was lying on Russ Smith's bed, which had been left unmade. It appeared Lisa had moved into her father's bedroom. The question was: had she moved into his bed?

Dylhoff immediately thought of a conversation he had with a former neighbor's child who had accompanied the Smiths on a summer vacation to Florida. "At night Russ would sleep with Lisa and I would share the second bed with Khris," the girl had said.

Based on the current living arrangements of Lisa and Russ Smith, detectives determined the child should be interviewed immediately. Since fathers are the third most likely child sex offenders behind stepfathers and mother's boyfriends, the search team's findings would have to be reported. The possibility of inappropriate behavior between Smith and his daughter could be excluded, or action could be taken at once to protect Lisa from what could prove to be an incestuous relationship.

Lisa Smith would be brought in for questioning as soon as Child Protective Services could be notified.

The Smith case was moving in directions investigators had not foreseen. They suspected Smith of foul play in his wife's disappearance, but now sexual abuse of a child and theft might be added to the list of Smith's possible crimes.

Chapter 11

Detective Palenick tabulated all the items taken by the Portage Police search team from the residence on Thunderbay. Copies of the property record and tabulation were left on the table in the living room for Russ Smith's review.

At Smith's request, he was paged at the number left with Palenick. He never returned the call.

Detective Dylhoff was apprehensive about the relationship between Russ Smith and his daughter, Lisa. It appeared Lisa had been sleeping in her father's bed for some time. Smith had dyed Lisa's hair on at least three occasions. Dylhoff felt overwhelming concern for the physical, as well as the emotional, well-being of Lisa Smith.

Experts in the field of child sexual abuse believe that incestuous parents often love their children, but put their own sexual/intimacy needs before the needs of their children. Sometimes, in cases like the Smiths, the incest is due to a crisis in their lives. The violation is more than sex. It's a breach of trust, a breaking of boundaries, and a profound attack on the child's sense of self.

Dylhoff felt it crucial to contact Child Protective Services at once. He placed the call to the supervisor of Child Protective Services, where he learned that caseworker Maureen Gallagher had been assigned the Smith case. The next day, Dylhoff and Gallagher made contact with Lisa at Angling Road Elementary School.

Gallagher and Lisa sat in a room by themselves. Although Dylhoff was unable to be physically in the room during the interview, he could hear what was said.

Gallagher, who had a relaxed manner, took a seat beside the small girl. Gallagher's large hands lay comfortably on top of the table, beside the tiny hands of the child. Gallagher spoke in a soft, nonthreatening tone, reassuring Lisa with every word. The two spent a few minutes in casual conversation. Lisa talked about getting makeup for Christmas the previous year and her mother letting her put it on for special occasions. She told Gallagher she had different colors of eye shadow and lip liner.

"My father lets me wear it and lets me wear something fancy. He buys my dresses and picks them out for me," Lisa said.

"Lisa, do you know the difference between the truth and a lie?" Gallagher asked.

"Sometimes I lie and sometimes I tell the truth," Lisa responded.

Gallagher broached the subject of the disappearance of Lisa's mother.

"Mommy was up the morning of September twenty-eighth. I got dressed, then went out and got on the bus and went to school. I also rode the bus home from school. When I got home, Daddy was there. He said that Mommy had left. I don't know where Mommy is living now," Lisa said.

"How did you and your mommy get along?" Gallagher asked.

"Good!" Lisa replied. "We went shopping together, out to eat, and to the gas station." Lisa's face brightened, reflecting fond memories of more pleasant times.

Lisa told Gallagher she was taking piano but discontinued the lessons after Christmas, claiming she wanted to take some time off. From another room Dylhoff wondered if Lisa dropped out of piano, an activity she seemingly loved, not because she wanted out but because her father didn't want to make the effort to get her to her lessons.

"What kinds of things did you do as a family?" Gallagher inquired.

"We would go to the movies, shopping, out to eat, and sometimes we'd go to the park," Lisa replied.

Lisa implied that her parents got along well most of the time, although they would also fight at times.

"Did your mommy have any men friends?" Gallagher prodded.

"Mommy used to have a friend by the name of Lyn; he's a man," Lisa answered. "I was in kindergarten and first grade. Sometimes Mommy would take me to Lyn's house to play with his two daughters. Daddy knew about Lyn and told Mommy he didn't want her to see him anymore. I knew Mommy was still seeing Lyn because sometimes she'd say she was going to the grocery store, and when she came back, she didn't have any groceries. I told Daddy [that] Mommy was lying. Mommy and Daddy got into a fight."

In the adjacent room Dylhoff rested his chin on his fist. Had Khris's relationship with Lyn, be it friendship or lovers, been the beginning of the end to the Smith marriage?

"How did you feel about that?" Gallagher inquired.

"Daddy and I were angry," Lisa answered.

Lisa told Gallagher that she knew of no other male friends her mother had; then she mentioned that her father had some new women friends.

Returning to the topic of the day Khris Smith disappeared, Lisa told Gallagher that her father had put a suitcase packed with her clothes (her own flowered overnight case), Buster, the bunny, and his cage, and a big black can in the back of his truck. Russ Smith had told his daughter her mother's clothes were in the barrel. Lisa had not questioned her father further.

Dylhoff ran his fingers through his thick brown hair. If Russ Smith planned to travel to Florida in search of his wife, why wouldn't he be taking a suitcase with extra clothing? The weather during late September in Florida was certainly balmier than that of southeastern Michigan or Ohio.

"Daddy let me read a note Mommy left, but I can't remember what it said," Lisa told Gallagher.

"Do you remember if your daddy had any cuts, scrapes, or bruises on his hands or arms?" Gallagher asked gently.

"No," Lisa replied.

"Did your grandparents ask about what was going on, or did you talk to them about your mommy?" Gallagher questioned.

"No. They didn't ask and we didn't talk about Mommy," Lisa said. She explained that her father had only been gone a couple of days before returning to her grandparents' Ohio home.

"He said that he couldn't find Mommy. I was very mad at Mommy for leaving. Daddy was mad too," Lisa commented.

Gallagher gently steered the conversation to the Smith household, specifically to the upstairs bathroom, where authorities believed Khris Smith may have been attacked by her husband.

"Which bathroom do you use in the house?" Gallagher asked.

"The bathroom in the hall, that was Mommy's and my bathroom," Lisa replied.

The child elaborated by saying that before she and her father left for Ohio, the walls in the bathroom were white. After her father picked her up and brought her back home, the bathroom looked different. The walls were a grayish white in color. The doors on the bathtub had also been changed, the original bubble glass doors replaced with clear-and-frosted striped doors. Lisa explained that most of the changes were made while she was in Ohio with her grandparents, but she had helped her father pick out and hang flowered wallpaper.

"Daddy didn't say why he changed the bathroom. He just wanted a change, so he did it," Lisa stated matter-of-factly.

"On the day you left for Grandma's in Ohio, were there any rooms you were not allowed to go into?" Gallagher asked.

"We have three bathrooms. I can use any bathroom I want," Lisa said with an air of insolence.

Again Gallagher slyly guided the conversation in the direction of her next inquiry. Lisa fell right into line, talking about how she would play dress-up and wear her mother's makeup when Khris was living at home.

"Now that Mommy's gone, I dress up in fancy dresses with makeup for Daddy," Lisa said. "And Daddy wanted my hair colored. He dyed it and my hair turned pumpkin orange. Daddy then took me to Siesta Salon and had it colored strawberry blond."

"Why did your father dye your hair?" Gallagher asked.

"He just wanted it changed," Lisa said. "I didn't want it done; he dragged me in to have it dyed. I told him I didn't want it done, but he told me I was going to do it anyway."

Based on information yielded by interviews, it was decided to remove Lisa Smith immediately from her home and place her into the custody of Protective Services. Lisa Smith would be living with a foster family until a formal hearing could be held to determine the best interest of the child.

While Dylhoff and the rest of the investigative team waited for the Protective Services hearing, they continued to field leads pertaining to Khris Smith's disappearance. As with any investigation, people with little information but a great deal of interest came forward.

One such person related a dream she had where a man was removing a brown garbage bag from the trunk of a car. As the man started to release the bag down into an opening between a concrete wall and the ground, she saw a woman's thigh through the side of the bag. She didn't get a good look at the man in her dream, but he had reddish hair.

Another dreamer described his vision to Detective Palenick. The caller had apparently dreamed that a man had been holding his wife in the basement against her will, then killed her. In his dream a construction

worker on a bulldozer was pushing dirt up against a wall
and noticed a piece of cloth rise from the ground. He
stopped, got off his tractor, and picked up the cloth. It
was only a small piece, igniting no cause for concern as
the dozer operator finished filling in the hole.

Although no relationship could be established between the Smith case and the visions of these or
others who phoned in, each one had to be heard and
evaluated for potential worth. Usually they were tips
of no evidentiary value, but one call worth a follow-up
came in.

Russ Smith had borrowed a friend's boat about the
time Khris Smith vanished. The boat belonged to
Terry LaFountain, one of Smith's coworkers.

Russ Smith missed his daughter very much. He also
feared what was being said between Lisa and the authorities. Smith had not been allowed to talk with Lisa
by phone or in person since the day Child Protective
Services had taken her away. For the child's safety, authorities declined to tell Smith where Lisa was living.
He intended to find a way to locate her whereabouts,
regardless of the measures he had to take. He wanted
to talk with her.

On January 16, nearly four months with no word of
Khris Smith, Dylhoff attended the scheduled hearing
for Lisa Smith at juvenile court. The hearing to determine if Lisa would go back to her father's house or
remain in foster care was to be mediated by Ann Har-
rison. Due to court scheduling, the hearing was reset
for January 25. Following the announced delay, Dylhoff
briefly spoke with caseworker Gallagher.

Maureen Gallagher handed Dylhoff a package. As

the detective looked at the small bra inside the bag, Gallagher also handed Dylhoff a box containing a black-handled filet knife in a leather sheath. Both the bra and the knife had been placed in Lisa's suitcase by her father.

Gallagher reported that the knife had been found in Lisa's bag, along with her clothes to be taken with her to her grandparents' in Ohio.

"According to Smith, the knife was a birthday gift for his father. However, when it was found in Lisa's bag, it was in an open box with no wrapping," Gallagher explained.

Dylhoff studied the knife carefully. He would send it to the lab to determine if any blood was on the handle or blade and whether or not it was human or animal. He noted that the knife appeared to have been used, not something someone would give as a birthday gift.

Before parting, Gallagher told Dylhoff she had set up a phone contact between Lisa and her father.

On his way back to the Portage PD, Dylhoff stopped by the residence of Donna Schuring, a neighbor of the Smiths on Thunderbay. Schuring had contacted Dylhoff, stating she had information pertaining to Russ and Lisa Smith.

When Dylhoff arrived at the Schuring residence, Donna told the detective that four days earlier before Lisa was taken into foster care, Lisa had been in their home to play with her daughter.

"We went out and did some errands. About seven P.M. I heard Lisa say to my daughter, 'Doesn't that tickle?' When I looked back, I saw Lisa with a twirling baton. She had put one end of it into my daughter's mouth and was turning it. I said, 'Lisa!' She let go of the baton and it fell onto the floor. Nothing more was said. Then at 8:30 P.M. when Russ came to pick Lisa up, I heard the girls go into my daughter's room and close the door. I heard it lock. I excused myself and knocked on the door and told the girls to unlock it. When my daughter opened the door, Lisa was back in the corner. She said, 'I don't want to go home.' She looked like she was going to cry and she seemed frightened. I talked with her a little bit and she finally came out and left with Russ."

Dylhoff listened attentively to Schuring's words. He hoped Lisa would feel safe in her new foster home.

"Lisa also had impetigo real bad sometime in October, all the way around her mouth and on her lips. She couldn't go to school for a day or two," Schuring stated.

Dylhoff thanked Donna Schuring for her call and asked her to get in touch if she thought of anything more or noticed anything strange at the Smith house.

On his way back to the Portage PD, Dylhoff recalled that Russ Smith had caller ID on his home phone. If Lisa placed the call to her father as planned, he would be able to obtain the phone number of the foster family and, with a little effort, could find her location. Dylhoff called and left a message for Gallagher to phone him as soon as possible.

Later that day, Smith entered the office of Jason Stevens, loss-prevention associate at Sears. Detective Dylhoff himself had dropped by Stevens's office only minutes earlier. Quickly the detective was able to conceal himself in a back room so that Smith didn't know he was present.

Smith wanted Stevens to research a phone number for him.

"I can't right now," Stevens said, telling Smith to get

back with him later. Only ten minutes passed before Smith was back in Stevens's office.

"Do you have the number?" Stevens asked.

Smith appeared anxious and impatient as he moved quickly inside the office. He pulled a small scrap of paper from his pocket, handing it to Stevens.

"Do you have a name to go with this?" Stevens inquired.

"All I have is the first name of Tom or Teresa," Smith replied. "I want to find out who they are and what their address is."

"Why do you need the information?" Stevens asked skeptically, his brow wrinkled.

"It's a situation with a customer. I believe the people were returning fraudulent batteries. They demanded cash. I've gone through the Sears in-house computer without any luck. I'd like you to contact the other anchor stores (Penney's, Hudson's, Mervyn's) to see if the phone number and names are on any of their records. I need the information as soon as possible," Smith insisted.

"It'll take me a little bit of time," Stevens told him.

Smith left Stevens's office, but he returned ten minutes later, only minutes after Dylhoff had slipped out with the phone number Smith earnestly sought.

"Have you found anything?" Smith asked anxiously.

"No, but you can use the cross-reference books we have," Stevens offered.

Smith began looking through all of the crisscross books offered by Stevens. Smith went through every index. Periodically he pulled a small white piece of paper out of his pocket, looked at a handwritten telephone number, then placed it back in his pocket.

After being unable to locate the information, Smith left the office in a huff.

When Dylhoff looked at the number Smith had given Stevens, he immediately placed a call to Gallagher. Dylhoff explained Smith had the phone number and was actively searching for Lisa's location. Gallagher informed the detective that the foster family had received three hang-up calls immediately after the scheduled phone call between Russ and Lisa. The family hadn't had any calls like that in the past. They assumed it was Russ Smith.

Although Smith had only been able to obtain the telephone number to the foster family, his persistence at pursuing the address was sure to net him what he wanted in a short time.

"It's my recommendation you move Lisa," Dylhoff told Gallagher. "It's possible that if Smith locates his daughter's address, he might attempt to pick her up."

A short time later, Gallagher advised Dylhoff that Lisa had been moved to another location a couple of miles away from the foster parents'. She felt certain Lisa would be safe.

Dylhoff didn't want to take the chance that Russ Smith would find Lisa, grab her, and run. He contacted the Kalamazoo Sheriff's Department, advising them of the situation. He gave them the address of the former foster parents and Lisa's new residence. Dylhoff asked that they keep an eye out for Smith, just in case he showed up in an attempt to kidnap his daughter.

Finally Dylhoff breathed a sigh of relief. For the time being, Lisa Smith was safe. It was up to the court to keep her out of harm's way.

Chapter 12

It had been five days since Russ Smith had seen his daughter. In addition to Jason Stevens, Smith spoke to Mindy Bushouse, the newest loss-prevention manager at the Portage, Michigan, store, in another attempt to locate Lisa. Bushouse refused, opting not to get involved in the situation between Smith, his daughter, and Protective Services. The day finally did come when Smith was able to see and speak to Lisa. Maureen Gallagher authorized a scheduled visit.

A broad grin lifted Smith's mustache as he saw Lisa's radiant face for the first time since she'd been taken from their home. The eyes of both father and child glistened at the emotional reunion, but Smith's happiness was short-lived.

The visitation didn't go as Smith had hoped. Chaperons were present the entire time, eliminating the privacy Smith had anticipated. He wanted to talk with Lisa alone, to hold her, and to kiss her without the watchful eyes and listening ears of authorities. Instead, father and daughter played games, drew pictures, and colored during the short, closely guarded visit.

Smith was more determined than ever to find Lisa's foster home.

* * *

Terry LaFountain had been employed in the automotive department at Sears for about thirty years. The fifty-seven-year-old loved fishing and had used his sixteen-foot outboard boat for years on the surrounding Michigan lakes.

On Thursday, September 29, the day after his wife disappeared, Russ Smith called LaFountain wanting to talk about Khris. Smith arrived at his friend's house in Plainwell about 10:00 P.M. He talked about his marital problems and how he believed Khris had left him for another man.

LaFountain listened attentively to Smith as he told him he was uncertain if he wanted Khris back or if he would be able to take her back if she returned. LaFountain encouraged Smith to try to salvage his marriage, to try to work things out.

The older man handed Smith two books, *Happiness: How to Find It* and *Building a Happy Family Life.* He advised Smith to read them. He believed they might help him with the decision concerning Khris and his marriage.

The next day, Smith asked LaFountain if he could rent his boat. "I want to get away and do some fishing to relax. To think the whole situation through," Smith said.

"I won't rent you the boat, but you're welcome to borrow it at no cost," LaFountain replied. He considered his boat a "community craft," often letting friends borrow it for their own use. The older vessel, a sixteen-foot Atlas Traveler with a 100hp Mercury outboard motor, showed years of wear with a variety of fiberglass patches on the sides and bottom. It was transported atop a sixteen-foot white trailer.

That evening, just as the last remnants of the sun

sank below the horizon, Smith drove the twenty miles to LaFountain's Plainwell house to hitch up the boat and trailer.

"I just need it for the weekend," Smith told his friend. "I'll get it back to you before the weekend is over."

Smith drove away from LaFountain's house, the boat and trailer following behind. The bed of Smith's truck was empty.

The next afternoon, as LaFountain worked in the Sears Auto Center, Smith stopped by.

"I'll bring the boat back to your house," Smith said.

"Just bring it back to the store. I can hook it up and take it home so you won't have to go all the way out to Plainwell," LaFountain offered.

Smith had had LaFountain's boat less than twenty-four hours. He didn't talk about fish he had caught, or if he had actually done any fishing, although he did mention going out on Gull Lake. LaFountain believed Smith had borrowed the boat, not to fish, but just to get away. He believed Smith had needed time to relax. Time to think. This belief was reinforced when Smith mentioned he had read one of the books LaFountain had given him.

In January, after learning about Smith borrowing Terry LaFountain's boat and going to Gull Lake the day after his wife's mysterious disappearance, Detective Dylhoff once again contacted Debbie and Tim Orosz. It had been four months since anyone had seen Khris Smith, but the Oroszes recalled the battered blue-and-white boat with fiberglass patch marks. It had been parked behind Smith's Dodge Dakota truck on the street in front of his house.

Debbie Orosz was positive she had seen the boat parked at the Smith's curb on September 29, the day after Khris left, the day Russ had talked with Tom Huss, and the day the Portage Police Department was first notified of suspicions surrounding Khris and Russ Smith.

In addition to Debbie Orosz, Tom Huss confirmed he'd seen a battered boat hooked up to Smith's truck the morning of September 29.

Randy Dylhoff's investigative instincts gnawed at him. He called Lieutenant Terry Vanstrien of the Kalamazoo County Sheriff's Department (KCSD). After discussing the Khris Smith case, Dylhoff told Vanstrien, "I think it's a possibility that Khris Smith's body might have been disposed of in Gull Lake."

"I'll have my officers check the lake out to see whether or not it would be feasible to attempt a sonar search right away or after the spring thaw," Vanstrien said.

The typical cold Michigan winter, with temperatures that dipped in the single digits, several feet of snow piled along roadways and shorelines, and thick layers of ice on ponds and shallow areas of lakes, made search efforts problematic. The recovery of a body would be arduous at best.

Dylhoff was beginning to feel the case coming together. He wanted to know where Smith went, whom he saw, and what he did. Upon the approval of his superiors, Dylhoff contacted Lieutenant Chet Wilson of Michigan State Investigative Resources. Wilson agreed to provide a four-person team that would tail Smith and monitor his activities.

In addition, Don Sewell, the store manager at Sears, advised they intended to put up a camera in the au-

tomotive garage to see if Smith brought in his vehicle
and took away merchandise from the store.

Smith would be unaware he was being watched
nearly every waking minute of his day. The surveillance would begin following the juvenile court
hearing on January 25. The hearing would determine
if Lisa Smith would be returned to her father's home
or remain in foster care.

The day of the hearing, Russ Smith was astonished
to see Kay Klein, Khris's mother, present. Adding to
Smith's surprise, Klein told Gallagher that she wanted
to be considered as a relative placement for Lisa.
Smith just wanted everyone to leave him and his
daughter alone. He wanted her back with him and his
patience for the situation was growing thin.

The hearing didn't net Smith the decision he
hoped for. Lisa would continue to live at the designated foster home for at least one more day. Judge
Carolyn Williams wanted time to talk personally with
Lisa. She intended to speak with Lisa the next morning and then make her decision on placement.

Frustrated and wallowing in self-pity, Russ Smith left
the hearing and drove to Pepper's, a topless bar on
Ravine near Douglas in Kalamazoo Township. Smith
drank beer, watched the dancers, and worried about
the interview between Lisa and the judge. To escape
the thoughts of court proceedings and an absent wife,
Smith engaged one of the dancers in conversation.

An hour after Smith entered Pepper's, the surveillance team watched from the cold interior of their car
as their subject emerged from the topless bar with an
unidentified white female. Smith drove to his house,
where both he and the woman stayed for over an
hour before the unnoticed watchers decided to call it

a night. They would pick up the Smith surveillance
the next day.

On the following afternoon Russ Smith heard from
Maureen Gallagher of Children's Protective Services.
He squeezed the phone tightly in his hand, his jaw
rigid, his body quaking slightly as he heard that Lisa
would remain in foster care for at least another three
weeks. At that time, Smith was told, a pretrial custody
hearing would be held. Adding to Smith's anxiety, his
mother-in-law had promised Gallagher she would be
present at the February 16 pretrial hearing.

Smith drove fast and erratically through the wet
streets of Portage. He stopped at Sears for a time,
then headed for an ATM at the local mall. At that
point the undercover team lost him for about an
hour, finally spotting his familiar red sports car at the
County Palace on King's Highway. The Michigan
State Police (MSP) agents went into the Palace to ob-
serve Smith. They sat at a table across the room and
watched as Smith drank a pitcher of beer, apparently
drowning his aggravation with the court system.

The night was growing late and it appeared Smith
would be at the Palace for a considerable time. The surveillance team decided to call it a night and go home.

The next day, the lead officer advised Dylhoff they
would return the following week to run another couple of days' surveillance. They hoped Smith would
make some personal contacts instead of just doing the
barhopping thing.

Meanwhile, Portage detectives continued with the
mundane search of Smith's credit card activity, phone
records, and work history. They learned that Smith,
once a gung ho Sears employee, had become detached

from his work. His former high company standards had grossly deteriorated.

On February 2, 1995, Detective Randy Dylhoff spoke with Jack Keyes, another of Russ Smith's neighbors. Keyes, who admitted he didn't know the Smiths well, characterized Khris as friendly and outgoing, always with a wave and a smile for him. Russ Smith, on the other hand, never acknowledged him and appeared cold and standoffish. As other neighbors had remarked, it was Khris who shoveled snow or did yard work. Russ Smith never appeared to be around.

Keyes told Dylhoff he noticed on September 28, the day of Khris Smith's disappearance, Khris running back and forth between a tan-colored car parked on the street and her house. She was throwing clothes and several pieces of luggage into the vehicle. Although Keyes couldn't hear what was said, Khris appeared to be yelling at someone as she went about her task. Keyes, thinking it was a family disturbance of some type, finished mowing his lawn and paid no further attention to what was going on at the Smith residence. He was certain it was on Wednesday, September 28, since he always mowed his lawn on Wednesdays.

The story gave Dylhoff reason for despair. He was certain Russ Smith was responsible for his wife's disappearance, yet Keyes's recollections conflicted with other known facts concerning Khris Smith's activities on the day in question.

But Dylhoff's instincts were reconfirmed when Keyes recalled seeing Russ Smith driving south on Thunderbay with a black fifty-five-gallon barrel in the back of his truck. The barrel had been tied down to keep it from falling over. Smith had also been pulling a boat behind his truck.

Keyes also remembered that when Smith returned after dark, he had slowed almost to a stop when he made the turn from French Bay onto Thunderbay. The barrel had no longer been in the back of the pickup.

Dylhoff knew it was time to call again on Terry LaFountain. Questions circled in his head. Did the boat show any signs of a barrel having been loaded in the craft? Were any stains visible, such as blood? Dylhoff drove the nearly twenty miles to Plainwell from Portage to inspect LaFountain's boat personally.

Dylhoff shivered as he stepped from his warm vehicle into the frigid February air. Smokelike vapors poured from his mouth as he circled the older fiberglass craft. He stopped, leaning down slightly to take a closer look at the top edge of the rail at the rear of the boat. Black scuff-marks marred the surface; they appeared to be some type of paint transfer. There were gouge marks in the fiberglass, but there was no black coloring in them. On the outside edge of the top rail, again in the rear of the boat, there were more black scuff marks. To Dylhoff's eye, it appeared that something black had been leaned against the top rail and that the object had rubbed against the rail.

Dylhoff took two small envelopes from his jacket pocket. He carefully scraped off the black transfers into the two separate envelopes. One contained the scrapings from the inside part of the rail, the other scrapings from the outside of the rail. As Dylhoff placed the envelopes in his pocket, he noticed that the boat was equipped with a working depth finder. A chill ran down Dylhoff's spine, not from the frigid air, but from the thought that Khristine Smith's body might be encased in a black fifty-five-gallon barrel at the bottom of Gull Lake.

Chapter 13

Eight days after the first surveillance of Russ Smith, the tailing team again tracked Smith's activities. They had no better luck than on their first attempt. Again Smith had spent most of his time at Pepper's, the County Palace, Déjà Vu, or other topless bars in the Kalamazoo area.

Bob Scott knew about Smith's newfound interest in exotic dancers. He had talked openly about them at work, had bragged about them.

"Do you want to see a picture of a girl I've taken out to dinner?" Smith had asked, a boyish grin across his face.

When Scott said he guessed so, Smith produced a photo of a naked girl who apparently was a dancer at the Mermaid Lounge. She had personally auto-graphed the picture for Smith, "To Russ."

Scott informed Dylhoff about the photo but was more concerned that Smith had made returns on five or six store items without receipts. He had returned a couple of Michelin truck tires, and although it was against store policy, he had demanded the $188 refund in cash. On another occasion, he had again demanded cash for one returned tire, refusing to give his driver's license to the store cashier.

Scott informed Dylhoff that Sears store personnel intended to look into the matter further.

Scott considered himself a good friend of Russ Smith's. His wife watched Lisa on nights that Smith had to work, as well as times when Smith went out. When Russ Smith told Scott about the day Khris left, Smith admitted they had argued over an affair Khris was having with another guy. He reported that she wanted to continue that relationship, as well as remain with Russ.

"He stated that the last time he saw her, she was walking down the road by herself. She didn't take anything with her," Scott told Dylhoff. But Scott said the second time he and Smith discussed Khris's leaving, Smith said she had packed some bags when she left. The variance of the stories had caused Scott to wonder about the truth concerning Khris Smith's departure.

Smith had also taken the tabulation of his property made by the police during the search of his residence to Sears.

"He showed it to me and made a comment as he pointed to the area where the document stated a rug from the garage steps was taken. He said he had had a roadkill deer in the back of his truck. There was a big spot of blood on the rug that was probably deer blood. He then said, 'That will throw them off,' and he started laughing. I couldn't believe he was making a big joke out of this whole incident," Scott told the detective.

Smith at first told Scott that Lisa wasn't having any trouble with Khris being gone because she hated her mother. He and Lisa had enjoyed going out to dinner, and Lisa had been going to the Discovery Zone. Then, in October, Smith said Lisa was having a little trouble sleeping at night, so he had moved all of her things into his room for a little while. Later, he told Scott that Lisa had moved in everything by herself.

Scott expressed concern that Russ's personality had started to change. He cut his hair short in the back, although he continued to comb it back in the front. He had also had his ear pierced.

"He told me he had made a bet with a friend on who would win the Super Bowl. He lost the bet, so he had to get his hair cut and his ear pierced and wear the earring for two weeks," Scott said. But Smith had kept the earring long after the two-week obligation.

Then there had been the photo of the nude dancer and Smith's boasting that they had had dinner together.

Scott told Dylhoff that he found it most unusual that Smith had made a comment when a police car had passed them on the road one day, saying, "See, they're following me and watching me." Smith also thought it was the lowest of dirty tricks that his daughter had been taken away. He suggested it was a plot to make him snap and talk to authorities about Khris. Smith, however, had stated that he had no intentions of talking to them now that they had taken his daughter away.

On a tip from Maureen Gallagher of Child Protective Services, Detective Dylhoff decided to meet with Teresa, the foster mother with whom Lisa Smith was staying. Dylhoff made an appointment to sit down with Teresa and talk about Lisa.

"Yesterday Lisa and I were talking. I had taken off my diamond ring and laid it on the table," Teresa began. "Lisa picked it up and began looking at it. She said she had a ring just like it that her daddy had given her. She said it was her mommy's. Lisa told me that when her daddy had left the house for a while, then when he came back, Mommy had cut the ring off her finger and it was laying on the table. She said the ring was in Ohio at her grandma's. She also said that there was some other jewelry, as well as other items, at Grandma's that belonged to her mother."

Teresa looked at Dylhoff with deep concern in her eyes. She spoke in a low voice. "Lisa said the reason her daddy gave her the things was because he told her that 'she was taking Mommy's place now.'"

Dylhoff could tell that Teresa was genuinely anxious about Lisa and the relationship with her father. The little girl was lucky to have someone who cared about her well-being, even if Russ and Lisa Smith were not appreciative.

Teresa felt strongly that Lisa knew more about what happened with her mother than she was telling.

"When Lisa first came to our house, she was terrified of the bathroom. She wouldn't go in it. The first few days she would hold her elimination for so long that she was almost in pain before she would finally go in and use the toilet. She would always want to leave the door open. She also didn't want to take a bath," Teresa explained, adding that Lisa had been there almost thirty days and she was just beginning to go into the bathroom alone.

Teresa told Dylhoff that although her husband was present in the home, she was the one who was most involved with Lisa. "I sense a lot of anger toward men coming from Lisa," Teresa said.

"I'd like to talk to Lisa this evening when she gets home from school," Dylhoff said.

Teresa assured the detective that there wouldn't be a problem, although she would have to advise Maureen Gallagher that he would be talking with Lisa. Dylhoff set 6:00 P.M. as the time he would return to the foster parents' residence to talk with Lisa.

At 6:00 P.M. sharp, Randy Dylhoff rang the doorbell at Lisa Smith's temporary residence. After a few minutes of cordial conversation, the detective, who towered over the little girl, sat down with Lisa and her foster mother in the living room/kitchen area. They began to talk about the day Lisa's mother left.

At first the child relived the events of September 28, just as she had done with Maureen Gallagher during their interview at Lisa's school. But this time when she mentioned her father instructing her to pack some of her things, she also revealed that he told her not to go into the bathroom.

"Which bathroom did he tell you not to go in?" Dylhoff asked gently.

"Mommy and I used the bathroom in the hall. That was the bathroom that Daddy told me not to go into," Lisa replied.

Lisa lowered her head as if in shame. "While Daddy was on the phone, I went to go into the bathroom to find out what was in there, but the door was locked. I know where the key is kept. I got it and opened the bathroom door."

Dylhoff's heart beat a little faster. The child was obviously in pain at revealing the secrets behind the door she was forbidden to open, but his excitement at learning what she had seen was rising within him.

"The bathroom was in a terrible mess," Lisa continued. "There were pieces of the wall lying on the floor. There was a large hole in the wall to the right as you walk in through the door."

"How big was the hole from the floor up toward the ceiling?" Dylhoff asked.

"From here to here," Lisa said as she put her hand down near the floor, then raised it approximately five feet high.

"How wide was the hole?" Dylhoff questioned.

With her arms, Lisa indicated an area approximately two to three feet wide.

"I closed the door and finished packing," Lisa said. "I told Daddy that I had looked in the bathroom. He got very angry and upset with me. That was a bad secret. I had to tell Daddy. It wasn't a good secret, like not telling about a surprise birthday party."

Dylhoff could see the guilt in the innocent girl's eyes. She had disobeyed her father and was having to live with the secret that he had hoped to hide behind the closed bathroom door.

"Daddy told me that Mommy got mad and kicked a hole in the wall. Do you know what else Mommy did?" Lisa asked the detective.

"No. What?" Dylhoff said.

"Mommy broke the shower spout off. She also broke the faucet handle that turns the water on and off. She broke the little lever by the drain that controls the drain." Lisa seemed puzzled by the condition of the shower area and appeared to wonder why her mother would have done such a thing.

"Not only was there a big hole in the wall, but the furnace was also broke," Lisa said.

"What do you mean, the furnace was broke?" Dylhoff inquired.

"That thing in the wall where the heat comes through?" she responded.

"The register?" Dylhoff asked.

"Yes. That was also broke."

Lisa continued by telling Dylhoff that she had packed two suitcases. One had all of her clothes in it and one of them had some of her clothes, along with a few clothes for her dad. When they got ready to leave, they took Buster, her rabbit, his cage, and a big black can, which was in the back of her father's truck. Her daddy had said that the can contained her mother's clothes. He was going to see if she needed them if he found her.

"Were there any other large containers in the back of the truck?" Dylhoff asked.

"No," Lisa responded.

She told the detective about her dad leaving her with her grandma Smith in Ohio and going to Florida to look for her mom. Lisa said that her dad told her he called home and her mom had picked up the phone, so he had returned to Portage. Smith had informed his daughter that when he got there, all he found was the cut wedding ring. Lisa thought she had stayed at her grandmother's about a week and that her dad had come a couple of times to see her.

"Do you know what your daddy did with the black can he had in the back of the truck?" Dylhoff asked.

"No."

"How big was the can?"

From the child's description, Dylhoff determined it was a big black fifty-five-gallon barrel.

"It had a metal top with a ring that held the top on," Lisa added. "When I got back home from Grandma's, the black barrel was in my room. I took some clothes out of it to play with."

"How many barrels were in the basement?" Dylhoff questioned.

"I think four. I think there were two metal barrels and two plasticlike garbage pails. One of the plastic garbage pails had Buster's food in it. But now there's only one metal barrel that has some of Mommy's clothes in it," Lisa said.

Lisa continued, telling Dylhoff she had three jewelry boxes, two that were hers and one of her mother's, given to her by her father.

"Mommy's jewelry box has all of Mommy's jewelry and earrings in it," Lisa said. "It even has Mommy's watch in it. Daddy gave me the diamond out of Mommy's ring. It's in the safe at Grandma Smith's in Ohio."

"Was there any jewelry that your mommy always wore?" Dylhoff asked.

"Yes," Lisa replied, "her wedding ring and her watch."

"Did your mother have more than one watch?" Dylhoff questioned.

"No."

The seven-year-old told Dylhoff that her birthday was in less than a month, on March 9. Lisa expressed her feelings that the best birthday present in the world would be for her mother to come back home.

Dylhoff's heart sank. The innocence of the little girl was touching. Like Lisa, he hoped that her mother would surprise her on her birthday, but Dylhoff was an experienced homicide detective. He knew that it wasn't possible for Khris Smith to return home.

"Daddy said that Mommy might come back and try to steal me. I don't want that to happen," Lisa said sadly.

"Are you afraid of your mother?" Dylhoff asked, remembering Smith's comments to a friend.

"No. We did lots of things together, and I miss her," Lisa said with sincerity.

"Did Mommy have any friends that came over or that she saw regularly?" Dylhoff asked.

"No."

Dylhoff asked the child about the previous summer, when her father was filling in for the regional manager and was gone from home for long stretches at a time. Lisa said that she and her mother had spent a lot of time together. They went shopping, out to eat, and did things jointly at home. She said Khris hadn't seen anyone during the time her father was away.

"Mommy saw a man a couple of years ago when I was in kindergarten. His name was Lyn. She and Daddy would argue about that. I haven't seen him, and Mommy hasn't seen him in a couple of years," Lisa explained.

Lisa told Dylhoff that she used to take piano lessons, dance lessons, and gymnastics. She said she didn't take any of the lessons anymore because it made things too busy for her and for her daddy. It was obvious Russ Smith was not only changing his lifestyle, but that of his daughter. From what the detective had heard about Khris Smith, he felt certain she would be displeased that her child wasn't involved with all the activities she had planned for Lisa.

Dylhoff spoke in a soft, fatherly voice as he told Lisa that his whole goal and focus in the investigation was to locate her mommy.

"If you recall anything else or think of anything else that I should know, tell your foster mom and we'll get together again and talk," Dylhoff said, a friendly smile on his face.

Lisa Smith looked into Dylhoff's eyes and said, "I miss my mommy and wish she'd come back."

Chapter 14

Russ Smith had reluctantly completed the psychological evaluation required by Children's Protective Services and the judge who would determine where his daughter would reside. Tests of this type can pinpoint a person's sexual preferences to the degree of determining the person's penchant as to preferred age and sex.

The Abel Assessment for sexual interest is the most widely used of these evaluations. Developed in 1995 by Dr. Gene G. Abel, the technology measures a person's sexual interests in twenty-two categories, with emphasis on his or her deviant sexual interest in children.

The noninvasive, two-component test is comprised of 160 slides depicting images of young boys and girls, male and female teenagers, and adult men and women that are rated by the participant as to how disgusted or aroused they are by looking at them. The second part of the evaluation is a lengthy questionnaire that asks about the person's interest in a variety of sexually deviant behaviors, such as fantasies, sexual thoughts, and conduct.

Another measure of sexual deviance is the penile plethysmograph (PPG). Some working in the treatment of sexual offenders crudely call it the "peter meter." Developed in Czechoslovakia, the device was

first used to prevent draft dodgers from claiming they
were gay just to avoid military duty.

The PPG measures changes in the circumference
of the penis. A stretchable band with mercury in it is
fitted around the subject's penis. The band is connected to a machine with a video screen and a data
recorder. Any changes in penis size, even those not
felt by the subject, are recorded while he views sexually suggestive or pornographic pictures, slides, or
movies. He may listen to audiotapes with descriptions
of such things as children being molested. Computer
software is used to develop graphs showing the degree
of arousal to each stimulus.

The PPG has been made a condition of parole for
certain sex offenders and has been used in sentencing decisions for sex offenders. It has even been given
to children as young as ten who had abused other
children. And in child custody cases, such as the one
Russ Smith faced, it helped to determine if a father
is or is not likely to abuse his own child.

The outcome of the pretrial at family court held on
February 16, 1993, was that the doctor's report supported sexual contact allegations and Lisa Smith would
remain in foster care pending the outcome of a trial.
Once again Russ Smith left the county court dejected.

Randy Dylhoff and the other Portage PD detectives
continued to work the Smith case, hoping for a break.
The fillet knife and samples taken from the bed of the
truck had been sent to an outside laboratory for testing.
To the team's disappointment, the knife, as well as the
rug from the garage steps, showed no signs of blood.

The credit checks fared no better. There had still

been no activity by Khristine Smith on any of the accounts she held in her name or held jointly with her husband. All cash withdrawals made from the accounts had been done so by Russell Smith.

Then Dylhoff played a long shot. Through the Michigan State Police he contacted PSYTEP Corporation, which produces satellite imaging for Michigan. Often they'd shoot the Portage area. According to PSYTEP, there were no photos taken during the night of September 28, 1994, when Khris Smith disappeared. At best, finding an image helpful in the Khris Smith investigation would be a crapshoot. If photos were available, they'd be able to tell the color of the vehicles, but not the makes or models. They would not be able to identify license plate numbers. They would be able to see people in the area, but would not be able to identify them. Dylhoff learned that only one or two inquiries out of ten produced results.

The cost of a query would be $300. If an image was located, it would be another $1,500 to $2,300 for processing the image. The government would then be contacted to see if there were any declassified photos or information available in the area. That would take four to six months. Dylhoff asked PSYTEP to send him the information for his review and consideration. The image service would make a hole in his investigative budget and the prospect of locating a vehicle or person via the satellite system seemed remote.

After Dylhoff hung up with PSYTEP, Tim Orosz called and advised that he had thought of something unusual that had happened at the Smiths' residence a couple of years before.

"Russ was showing me his gun collection when he pulled out a small wooden case with blue lining. He

said, 'I've got something to show you.' As he opened
the box, I saw a silver or chrome-colored cylinder that
was about two or two-and-a-half inches long with holes
in it. It looked like a gun silencer. I asked Russ, 'What
the hell do you got that thing for?' and he just blew
it off."

Tim also advised Dylhoff that he still had a car radio
purchased from Smith for $25 that was still in the box.
He promised to get back with the detective to provide
the serial number to the radio.

Lisa Smith sat quietly on the living-room sofa as
Randy Dylhoff entered her temporary home. Tucked
under one arm was a photo album Lisa recognized;
under the other was a bag containing an unknown
object.

Dylhoff had already reprinted the negatives found
in the album during their search. The photos of the
bathroom prior to Smith's renovation and those
taken afterward had been inserted in the pages of the
album.

Lisa told the detective that her mother had taken
all the photos, other than the two of the remodeled
bathroom. She said her father had taken those.

In going through the pictures, Dylhoff noticed
wreaths and plants that were not in the home when
searched by the investigative team. Lisa told the detective they had been sold, perhaps in a garage sale. Many
of the personal touches Khris had made to the home
had disappeared, just as Khris herself had done.

"Lisa, I want you to go over again what happened
when you got home from school the day your mommy
came up missing," Dylhoff said delicately. The big

Khristine Klein Smith as a junior at Elida High School in 1984.

The Smiths—Russ, Lisa, and Khris—appeared to be the perfect family.
(Courtesy of CCCCAT)

The Smith house in Portage, Michigan. *(Courtesy of CCCCAT)*

The Smith family with their boat. *(Courtesy of Portage Police Dept.)*

Detective Randy Dylhoff of the Portage, Michigan Police Department was the first officer to investigate the disappearance of Khristine Smith. *(Author's photo)*

One of the photos of Khris Smith found by Randy Dylhoff in the Smith trash can had been torn in several pieces. *(Courtesy of CCCCAT)*

Neighbors Tim and Debbie Orosz helped police investigate Khris's disappearance. *(Author's photo)*

The upstairs bathroom in the Smith house appeared to be in perfect condition following Khris Smith's disappearance. *(Courtesy of CCCCAT)*

Investigators discovered another photo of the upstairs bathroom, revealing that the room had been recently remodeled. *(Courtesy of CCCCAT)*

Khris Smith's car remained in the family garage after her disappearance. *(Courtesy of CCCCAT)*

Detectives found merchandise stolen from Sears in the basement of the Smith house. *(Courtesy of CCCCAT)*

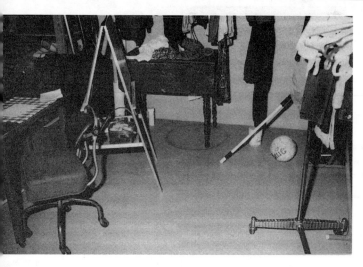

The Smith's basement floor had a circular stain where a 55-gallon barrel had been removed. *(Courtesy of CCCCAT)*

Lisa Smith's closet was nearly bare when searched by Portage PD detectives. Her clothes were later located in her father's closet. *(Courtesy of CCCCAT)*

Detective Dylhoff searched the boat that Smith borrowed from a friend the day after his wife's disappearance. Dylhoff believed Smith used the boat to dispose of his wife's body. *(Courtesy of CCCCAT)*

Detective Mike Werkema presented the case of Khristine Smith's disappearance and possible homicide to the newly formed Kalamazoo cold case squad. *(Author's photo)*

The Cold Case Career Criminal Apprehension Team comprised men
from various agencies in Kalamazoo County, Michigan:
Richard Mattison, Mike Brown, Captain Dan Weston,
Mike Werkema, Ron Petroski, and Greg Hunter.
(Courtesy of CCCCAT)

The new owners of the Smith house granted permission to the
CCCCAT to dismantle the bathroom in an effort to find evidence
of foul play. *(Courtesy of CCCCAT)*

Crime scene investigators removed the flooring from the bathroom in an attempt to find blood evidence. *(Courtesy of CCCCAT)*

Crime scene technicians used special light to search for clues.
(Courtesy of CCCCAT)

In the bathroom, investigators found rags believed to contain blood.
(Courtesy of CCCCAT)

Dr. Sundick and his students from Western Michigan University
searched for evidence in the backyard of the Smith property.
(Courtesy of CCCCAT)

Mike Werkema met with Roger and Linda Smith, along with their granddaughter Lisa, in an effort to solicit their help.
(Courtesy of CCCCAT)

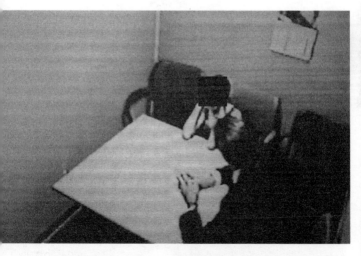

Detective Mike Brown met privately with Lisa Smith, encouraging her to reveal what she knew about her mother's disappearance.
(Courtesy of CCCCAT)

KALAMAZOO COUNTY SHERIFF

55030004
RUSSELL
LEE
SMITH
05/20/62

Height   Weight
601   195

7536 LOOP ST

Russ Smith was picked up in Florida, taken to Michigan, booked into the Kalamazoo County Jail, and charged with murder.
(Courtesy of CCCCAT)

Russ Smith accompanied Detective Richard Mattison and divers on a search for Khristine's body. *(Courtesy of CCCCAT)*

Russ Smith was unsuccessful at finding the barrel he claimed held his wife's body. *(Courtesy of CCCCAT)*

Mike Werkema believed Russ Smith may have disposed of his wife's body in the funeral home and crematory behind his parent's Ohio home. *(Courtesy of CCCCAT)*

Inside the crematory, Smith may have used one of the tools on this tool board to remove his wife's wedding ring.
(Courtesy of CCCCAT)

When he and Khris had made arrangements for their own funerals, Smith had been shown the operation of the cremation oven.
(Courtesy of CCCCAT)

Smith was familiar with these crematory oven controls.
(Courtesy of CCCCAT)

Mike Werkema and others believe the body of Khristine Smith may have been turned to ash in this cremation oven.
(Courtesy of CCCCAT)

Stuart Fenton, Assistant Prosecuting Attorney, presented the state's case, gaining a conviction of murder for Smith. *(Author's photo)*

Khristine Smith
12-17-66 to 9-28-1994
(Courtesy of CCCCAT)

man didn't want to intimidate the child or scare her, but he had to find out everything she knew in conjunction with her mother.

Lisa avoided the eyes of the discerning detective as she told him that her father had been on the phone and he'd told her to go pack her clothes and not to go into the bathroom in the hall.

"What bathroom was that?" Dylhoff asked once again.

"The one that Mommy and I used," Lisa replied. The young child explained how she had disobeyed her father by getting a stool and standing on it to retrieve the key kept on the ledge above the bathroom door. She had unlocked the door and put the key back on the ledge.

"Was it a regular-shaped key?" Dylhoff asked.

"It was shaped like a candy cane and you just pushed it in the hole on the outside of the door," Lisa explained.

"There were different objects on the sink in the photograph. Were those items on the sink or on the floor?" Dylhoff inquired.

"They were on the sink. There was a big hole in the wall and pieces of the wall lying on the floor. There were also cracks in the wall. Daddy had taken a scraper and scraped the wall over the cracks," Lisa stated.

Dylhoff handed the child a photo of the bathroom prior to the day her mother disappeared. The photo depicted the shower door slid all the way to the left, which was in the front of the tub, where the faucet was. Lisa stated that on the day her mommy left, the door was all the way to the right and she could see that the faucet and showerhead had been broken off.

"What about the lever for the drain?" Dylhoff asked.

"It was broken too," Lisa answered as she pointed to

the waterspout in the photo and added, "and that thing was broken." She couldn't recall whether or not the faucet and other tub fixtures were in the tub when she was in the bathroom.

"Daddy told me Mommy got mad and kicked the hole in the wall," Lisa explained.

"Was there anything in the bathroom that indicated your mommy might have gotten hurt?" Dylhoff asked.

"No. I didn't see any blood or anything. The only thing Mommy might have hurt was her foot when she kicked the wall," Lisa answered innocently.

Dylhoff asked about the cabinet above the toilet and the mirror by the sink. Lisa assured him they were still attached to the wall when she secretly entered the bathroom against her father's instructions.

Again, as she had in their prior conversation, Lisa told the policeman that her father had been angry with her for going into the bathroom.

Dylhoff was certain something more had happened to Khris Smith than becoming angry and kicking a wall. He was convinced she hadn't left the bathroom alive. He even believed he knew how her body had been transported from the house, but Dylhoff remained uncertain of just how Khris Smith died.

As if in a diversionary move, Lisa informed Dylhoff that her father had gotten her a big chocolate-candy Kiss for Valentine's Day; then she jumped up to run to her room to get it. She arrived back in the living room, smiling as she proudly showed off her Kiss. Lisa had also brought out her toy jewelry box and showed the policeman her prized children's jewelry collection.

"I also have the diamond out of Mommy's ring," she said with a grin. "It had one big diamond in the middle and a little diamond on each side. Mommy cut it off her finger and Daddy gave me the diamond out of it." Lisa didn't know where the ring was, but she told Dylhoff the diamond was at her grandparents' house in Ohio.

Sadness crept into the naive eyes of the seven-year-old. "I miss my mommy and wish she would come back home. My daddy wishes she would come home too."

Dylhoff's heart sank as he took a deep breath. He wished her mommy would return as well, but he held no hope for Khris Smith's return.

"I'm doing everything I can to locate your mommy for you," Dylhoff said as reassuringly as possible. "How are things going at school? Are the kids leaving you alone with everything that's going on with you?"

"Most of them are, but there's a couple of them who said that they think my daddy killed my mommy. They said they read it in the newspaper," Lisa said, sadness lacing her voice.

"What do you think?" Dylhoff asked gently.

"My daddy only kills deer," Lisa insisted.

It was February 27. In only ten days, Lisa Smith would turn eight years old. Dylhoff opened the sack he had brought and pulled out a plush animal. He handed the clear-eyed child a Portage Police Department teddy bear donated by the Portage Exchange Club. The bears had been given as presents to children under circumstances of trauma. The bears were a little something to comfort them and give them a degree of pleasure, an object to hold on to when tears swelled in their eyes and their hearts ached from loss and confusion.

A broad grin crossed Lisa's chaste face as she clung tightly to the soft bear. "I collect stuffed animals. Thank you very much," Lisa said with eyes that glistened with unspent tears.

Chapter 15

Based on the information gained from his interview with Lisa Smith, indicating the exact area of damage to the Smith hall bathroom, Dylhoff requested yet another search warrant. While waiting for the warrant to be signed, Russ Smith appeared at the Portage PD.

Smith had received a brochure and invitation from Yarrow, a center for personal growth and professional development in Augusta, Michigan. The brochure, addressed to Mrs. Khris Smith, advertised a "Wild Women Weekend." The notebook-size, tri-folded piece of paper encouraged the creative and intuitive power within by using myth metaphor, meditation, fairy tales, and ritual.

If Khris Smith had requested the brochure and entertained the idea of attending the "Wild Women Weekend," she hadn't told her husband. Russ Smith denied knowing anything about Yarrow.

"Russ, we need you back at the house," Dylhoff stated after making a copy of the brochure.

"Why?" Smith asked, obviously surprised and somewhat irritated.

"We have a search warrant," Dylhoff answered.

After assuring Smith he could first contact his attorney, Dylhoff left to wait at the Smith residence for Russ Smith to arrive.

The six-man search team entered the house through the garage door. A black steel fifty-five-gallon barrel was located in the basement of the house. A paint sample was carefully scraped off and dropped into a clear plastic Baggie to be taken to the lab for analysis. They would have to wait for the lab results to know if the paint sample matched the scrape taken from Smith's friend's boat.

The men entered the house, crossing the parquet flooring of the entry to climb the stairs to the second-floor bathroom. The walls of the house were painted white with natural wood trim around the doors and baseboards.

Upstairs, two members of the search team began inspecting the bathroom once used by Khris Smith. The wallpaper was carefully removed from the area of the bathroom where Lisa had indicated the wall had been damaged. Beneath the dubious covering of the paper, seams were visible where the drywall had been replaced. The drywall was carefully cut in the area of the seam opening, 59½ inches high and 45½ inches long. An officer, dressed in a white jumpsuit and wearing goggles, carefully dusted the walls with a fine brush.

Once inside the partition, searchers could clearly see that the original drywall had been glued to the studs. Dressed all in black, including a ball cap and goggles, an officer carefully inspected the interior walls with a black light. Spots of old glue were visible on the studs behind the wall that had been replaced, along with several smudge marks on the inside of the wall. The men carefully removed portions of the stained drywall for testing. They would later learn that the stain they suspected to be blood was not.

Looking closely between the wall and shower enclosure, they found a piece of fiberglass tub, which they marked and tagged as evidence. Also marked as evidence for testing were a small piece of drywall still glued to a stud, a larger section of the original drywall, a small piece of reddish brown material appearing to be a piece of skin or bone fragment, drywall with indentations, and what appeared to be a strand of hair located where the floor and wall joined. A mist of luminol was sprayed inside the shower and wall, with the hope that any blood splatters, regardless of how small, would appear.

It was obvious to search team members that something had occurred in the small interior room of the Smith home causing Russ Smith to alter the original construction. In a house that was only two years old, the chance of rotting wood or defective construction was minimal. They believed more than ever that a violent act had taken place in the upstairs bathroom of the Smith home.

Looking for evidence to support their theory, they removed the toilet, leaving the closet flange and wax ring. The area was scrutinized for any signs of blood.

The search team moved meticulously through the bathroom, removing the brown vanity, the sink, and the switchplates from the wall. The over-the-vanity brass light fixture with four frosted flair-shaped globes was taken down, and both the wall and fixture were examined for blood trace evidence.

Detective Dylhoff was busy checking other evidence. He went to Nuvision, the optical store where Khris Smith had obtained her eye exam and corrective lens. Khris's vision tested at -450. She was extremely nearsighted and would definitely have to wear her contacts or glasses in order to drive or do much else. Most often Khris chose to wear her hard contact lenses with a slight gray tint. The optometrist had suggested the light shading, not to enhance or change the color of her eyes, but so it would be easier for Khris to locate a lens if one was dropped on the floor. When not in contacts, Khris had a pair of lilac pink plastic frames with rose-tinted lenses.

On August 3, 1994, little more than a month before her disappearance, Khris had Nuvision clean and polish her contacts. That was the last time she had been seen at the optical shop. She hadn't checked in for additional contacts, hadn't needed any adjustments to her glasses.

After speaking to the staff at Nuvision, Dylhoff spoke with Dan Stevens at Dylhoff's office. Stevens, a close friend and employee of Smith's, described both Khris and Russ Smith to Dylhoff quite differently than their neighbors did.

"I had borrowed a children's videotape from the Smiths and told them I'd have it back by four P.M. a couple of days later. I didn't make it back on time and at five P.M. Khris Smith was at my door. She yelled at me about not returning the tape," Stevens said.

He stated that Khris was a "clean fanatic" who refused to let Russ change the oil or sand a car he was restoring in the garage.

In contrast, Stevens characterized Russ Smith as a husband who went out of his way to make his wife happy and to do things for her.

"I point-blank asked if Russ did anything to Khris," Stevens told the detective. "He said, 'I swear I don't know where she's at. I didn't kill her. I'm not a killer.'"

* * *

In February 1995 Raquel Owens was laid off from her job. Feeling lonely and somewhat depressed, she decided to place an ad in the *Kalamazoo Gazette*'s personals section. She hoped contact with a new man would lift her spirits. Shortly after placing the ad, Raquel received a call from Russ Smith. He left his name and a number where he could be reached.

The initial conversation between Raquel and Smith seemed more like a fact-finding mission than a casual introduction. She asked why he had answered the ad, to which he replied, "It intrigued me." She asked if he was married, to which he had responded, "No." He also denied having any children.

Smith let Raquel know he was originally from Ohio, had worked for Sears since he was eighteen years old, and was employed as the automotive manager. When asked what he looked like, Smith told his perspective date he was *GQ*-looking, making reference to the male models in *Gentleman's Quarterly*, an image that didn't quite fit his job or income status.

Raquel described herself as blond with brown eyes. "Do you dye your hair?" Smith asked.

"Yes, I do. I'm naturally brown-haired," Raquel replied.

The brief conversation quickly turned to his enjoyment of tanning and the fact that he owned his own tanning bed. He bragged about his new Mustang GT, then asked Raquel what type of champagne she liked.

"Asti Spumante," Raquel replied.

"I like that too," Smith declared, adding, "I always keep a couple of bottles in my trunk."

Through the conversation Raquel began experiencing a sense of apprehension. There was something about Smith that made her uneasy. She felt he was a little strange. She warned herself to be cautious.

"I don't have to go out with you if I don't want to," Raquel told Smith. "You don't know my phone number."

Smith's voice reflected a sly satisfaction, "I have your phone number on my caller ID."

Although the fact that Russ Smith took obvious pleasure in knowing her number made her nervous, in the end Raquel decided it wouldn't do any harm to see the man.

Smith arrived the following night with a bottle of champagne and a single rose. As Raquel opened the door of her apartment, Smith's first words were, "On first impressions, you are very beautiful."

The comment caught Raquel off guard. It had even scared her a bit. Smith was handsome and well dressed, but he made her uneasy.

"Let's have a drink before dinner," Smith said with a smile, holding the bottle of bubbly in his raised hand.

Raquel reluctantly let her new suitor inside and watched as he popped the cork on the green glass bottle. They decided on dinner at Chianti, a restaurant behind the Player's Pub on Stadium Drive.

Dinner was pleasant, filled with benign conversation. When asked what she wanted to do after dinner, Raquel suggested a movie. "We can go back to my place and call the theater to find out what shows are playing and when they start," Raquel suggested, her apartment being close by.

"Do you mind going to my house? I want to show it to you," Smith countered.

Raquel didn't have a problem going to his house. It would give her an opportunity to look around, to see how Russ Smith actually lived. Her first impression was that he had a lot of money. He had asked if she liked men who wore jewelry, pulling back his collar to reveal a gold necklace, and bringing up his arm to display bracelets and gold rings. He even had a pierced ear. She wondered, though, if Smith was a "mama's boy" when he expressed his concern that his mother didn't know about the earring and that he was worried about how she would react to it. It was an apprehension that seemed a bit strange for a man in his thirties.

Raquel was relieved when Smith finally steered his Mustang into his driveway on Thunderbay. He had frightened her with his driving, showing off the speed of the new Mustang and the maneuverability by darting in and out of traffic, actions reminiscent of a teenage boy with his first set of wheels. She breathed a sigh of relief as he pulled into his garage; then Raquel noticed a second car parked in the adjoining bay.

"It's my winter beater," Smith explained. Raquel thought it was a good idea, considering how he drove his sports car, to have a backup. Many people in Michigan had second cars, often battered, to drive during the winter months when ice and mounds of snow covered roadways, making travel treacherous.

Inside Smith's house Russ held the phone receiver to his ear as he called off the movies showing at the local theater and the times for each viewing. When Smith mentioned *The Lion King,* Raquel said she'd never seen it and would enjoy the lighthearted animated feature. Smith, however, wanted to see *Murder in the First.* So, *Murder in the First* it was.

Raquel and Smith shared another bottle of champagne in the family room of his house. Smith had wanted to set the mood for romance by lighting a fire, envisioning their two faces aglow in the light of the orange-and-yellow flames as they danced in syncopated rhythm. Raquel protested, rationally stating that it was a mere ten to fifteen minutes before they would leave for the theater. Smith spent that time showing Raquel around the house, never leaving the first floor, avoiding both the basement and second-floor rooms.

Raquel noticed the number of dried flowers and wreath decorations throughout the living area and commented on how nicely decorated Smith's home appeared.

"Did a woman help you with it?" Raquel asked, thinking the type of adornments had a definite female touch.

"No," Smith replied. "I did it myself."

In talking about his house, Smith bragged that it had four bedrooms and that if he were ever to leave Sears, the company would buy his house from him.

On their way to the theater, Smith drove past the Courtyard Apartments on Constitution Avenue. His date commented that she would be baby-sitting at the complex the following morning. It was an innocuous comment, an attempt at causal conversation rather than information to be filed for later use.

After the movie Smith drove Raquel to her apartment. Sitting in the front seat of the red Mustang, Smith asked Raquel if she had plans for Valentine's Day. "I have nothing else to do and no one to do anything with on that day," Smith stated.

It wasn't exactly the tender or appealing invitation one might expect for a Valentine's Day date. Raquel avoided making any definite plans with Smith. Even after spending several hours with him that evening, she was still uncertain of him. Something about him still troubled her.

The next day, Raquel arrived at her baby-sitting job in the Courtyard Apartments as planned. When her job was done and she left the apartment to get into her vehicle, she saw Smith's car parked next to hers in the lot. Raquel spotted Smith walking toward some of the town houses. Seeing him there was disturbing. It was almost as if he were stalking her.

"Russ!" Raquel yelled across the span of cars.

Smith turned, smiled, and walked back toward Raquel.

"What are you doing here?" she asked nervously, wondering why he would try to hunt her down.

"I came looking for you. I was going to go town house to town house until I found you," Smith said, a grin turning the corners of his mustache upward. "I want to know when we're going to see each other again."

Raquel's eyes darted around the apartment complex. She nervously pulled her coat closer around her suddenly trembling body. "I have some other things going on and I'll have to get back with you," Owens said. "But you left your gloves at my apartment when you were there last night. I'll get back with you about when you can come pick them up."

With that comment, Raquel Owens was gone.

Later, Raquel telephoned Smith. She told him she was dating someone else and no longer wanted to see him. She advised Smith to drop by and pick up his gloves. A short time later, Smith arrived at Owens's apartment. Her roommate answered the door.

"If your roommate or anyone here wants to get together, just give me a call," Smith said with a grin and
a wave as he walked away from the apartment.

Raquel Owens was a name detectives investigating
the Smith case hadn't heard until she contacted the
Portage PD. She had a gut fear of Smith that intensified when she realized he had been in the papers in
connection with his wife's disappearance. When she
mentioned to Detective Dylhoff she had dated Smith,
his interest had piqued.

When Owens was finished relaying the story to Dylhoff, she told him it had been the first time she had ever
placed a personal ad in the newspaper and it would certainly be her last. It had also been the first date with
anyone who responded to the ad. Raquel Owens declined any offers of dates after the one with Russ Smith.

Russ Smith was weary from the nerve-racking pressure of being a suspect in the disappearance of his wife.
He continually sensed the presence of the police, even
when they were nowhere around. Although he tried to
maintain a normal life, Russ Smith feared that at any
moment he would be arrested for Khris's murder.

On March 9, 1995, the day of Lisa's eighth birthday,
Smith heard a knock on the door. Peering through an
upstairs window, Smith saw the tall, leggy figure of Detective Randy Dylhoff standing on the porch. Smith
froze. Was Dylhoff there to arrest him for Khris's murder? Without a sound he stepped back from the
window. He didn't speak. He didn't move. Once he
heard the detective start his engine and drive away,
Smith took in a deep breath and released it in a long
sigh of relief.

Smith waited ten minutes after Dylhoff's departure before he opened the garage door and drove off. Minutes later, he phoned Detective Palenick at the Portage PD.

"I want to know if there's a warrant for my arrest," Smith demanded. "A neighbor called and said the police were back at the house looking around."

Oblivious that Dylhoff had visited the Smith residence to ask if Lisa may have received a birthday card from her mother, Palenick assured Smith he was unaware of any type of warrant or any contact made at his residence by their department. Smith relaxed. He wanted to believe Dylhoff was on one of his all-too-familiar "fishing" expeditions.

Smith's sense of calm was quickly erased in March 1995. Standing before a Kalamazoo County judge, Smith was arraigned on four felony counts of embezzlement from Sears. Absent was his engaging smile, his air of confidence. His head lowered, Smith stood mute before the court. Disbelief and anger marred his face as he shook his head gently when the judge set bond at $10,000.

Smith's world continued to crumble.

Following the arraignment, Dylhoff transported Smith from the Portage PD's jail to the Kalamazoo County Sheriff's Department in his unmarked Portage PD vehicle. Their conversation was casual. Dylhoff's only question was "When do you think all of this is going to end?"

"Soon, I hope," Smith replied with a groan, expressing his displeasure at a bond he felt excessive. "I'm getting screwed by the system."

As the relaxed dialogue between Dylhoff and Smith continued, Smith frequently asked if the conversation was being recorded. Dylhoff repeatedly assured him it was not.

"Is this just a Russ and Randy talk?" Smith inquired.

"Yes," Dylhoff stated as he pulled into the sheriff's department receiving area.

As the two men, near in age and similar in physical stature, sat in the detective's car, they continued to talk.

"What types of physical evidence do you have pertaining to Khris's disappearance?" Smith asked, adding, "It's probably very little, if any."

Careful not to compromise the investigation, the cop continued to talk with the suspect, but he didn't really answer the question. Smith asked if they could possibly go somewhere and get a soda. "I'm getting a little claustrophobic sitting in the car in this garage," Smith said.

"I don't see any problem with that," Dylhoff responded as he started the car and began backing out of the sheriff's receiving area.

Dylhoff headed for the nearest drive-through, a local Hot & Now on Sprinkle Road. After getting the drinks, Dylhoff guided the vehicle into a nearby parking lot a few businesses away, then cut the engine. It was obvious Smith had something on his mind and Dylhoff was anxious to listen. He pushed the record button on his tape recorder.

Dylhoff sipped his soda patiently as Smith frequently stated he couldn't believe he was talking with him. "I've never opened up to anyone like this before," Smith stated.

Dylhoff's cool eyes hid the contempt he felt for the man he was certain had killed his wife, the man he

suspected of sexually assaulting his own daughter. Dylhoff remained cool, encouraging Smith to open up,
ask questions, and talk freely about Khris, their relationship, and the day he claimed she disappeared. To
keep Smith talking, Dylhoff didn't stop to read Smith
his Miranda rights.

"Where does this rate in Portage crimes? Is it in the
top ten? Maybe even the top three?" Smith asked, a
gleam of what Dylhoff interpreted as satisfaction in
his eye.

Dylhoff wanted to throw his drink out the window
and punch Smith in the mouth. The man sitting next
to him was so cold, so unfeeling. He was obviously
more concerned with the enormity of the crime in
terms of importance—his importance—than the
crime itself. Where was his remorse, his guilt at taking
the life of the beautiful young mother of his child?
Dylhoff held his tongue and let Smith continue.

"After all this is said and done, we ought to get together and write a book," Smith said.

Dylhoff cringed at the words. He had no intentions
of spending any more time with Smith than necessary
to prove him a killer. Smith's arrogance and high opinion of himself was nearly intolerable, but Dylhoff knew
he had to use Smith's narcissism to his advantage.

Dylhoff looked at Smith through veiled sincerity.
"I'm aware you're a nice person," Dylhoff said. "I
know you are a caring, considerate person, a people
person. I knew it would just be a matter of time before
you would have to talk to somebody about the deal
with Khris."

"I don't think so," Smith said coyly. "I feel I could
live the rest of my life without telling anybody anything. I've already paid the price the last eight years."

Dylhoff knew Smith was referring to the number of years he and Khris had been married. And, regardless of his comment, Dylhoff was certain Smith needed to talk.

Smith asked what the lab had found on the piece of carpet they had taken from the step in his garage, then added, "You must have been really disappointed because the only thing that was on that was deer blood and some red spray paint."

Deer blood and red spray paint. Smith had not only attempted to throw them off the path, he had taken great pleasure in the effort.

"You didn't get anything out of the bathroom because there was nothing there," Smith said confidently. "You will never find what you're looking for. I hold the key."

Dylhoff let Smith go on. Through his arrogance the suspect was confessing. Dylhoff's instincts had been right all along. Russ Smith had killed his wife.

Dylhoff listened as Smith admitted that he had thought about suicide but believed it to be the coward's way out. He confided that the only concern he had was for his daughter. Lisa was his only reason for continuing to live. Although Dylhoff knew about Smith's frequent visits to the topless bars and taking women to his home, presumably for sex, the detective listened attentively as Smith reported that he had only been with a woman once since Khris had been gone, that he no longer had the "urge."

Few would have believed that statement. If Russ Smith hadn't wanted to attract women, why had he cut his hair, gotten an earring, lost weight, and bought a sports car? Some may have attributed it to a midlife crisis, but from the clubs he frequented and the personal newspaper ads he had run, it was apparent that Russ Smith had retained all the sexual urges he had always felt.

"What was the officer talking about who was initially going to transport me?" Smith asked, referring to Officer Babel, who had originally been assigned the task of taking Smith, along with a number of other persons, to the Kalamazoo County Jail. "He said something about driving past the area of Highway 131 and Milham and Atwater Pond."

"I don't know what you're talking about," Dylhoff said.

"It would be a waste of manpower hours to look there," Smith said, a smirk on his face.

"Russ, we think she's in the water somewhere," the detective stated.

"You're wasting your time; it's a waste of manpower hours," Smith repeated. "You're never going to find what you are looking for. *I* don't even know where she is now."

Smith was playing a cat-and-mouse game, one Dylhoff was forced to participate in if he wanted Smith to continue to talk.

Smith commented that he believed investigators had probably located his truck and, again, that they had more than likely not found anything other than deer blood and pieces of the old fiberglass tub and shower.

Dylhoff sipped his soda as he contemplated his next move. Out of the blue, Smith said, "How is your department with ballistics analysis? Who does them?"

"They're usually done through the state crime lab. Why?" Dylhoff asked. No one had mentioned ballistics or even the possibility that Khris Smith had died by gunshot. But Smith didn't reply.

"I have three basic requests," Smith stated firmly. "Lisa's welfare, that she be placed either with my parents or my brother or sister, and that I'll get an appropriate charge."

"What do you think is an appropriate charge?" Dylhoff asked as he moved Smith closer to a full confession.

"Possibly manslaughter," Smith stated. He felt comfortable with Dylhoff. Free to talk in indirect terms, if not specifics.

Smith felt he had been "screwed" by the system in family court and deemed the bond inappropriate on the embezzlement charge. He claimed that he had been told if he pleaded no contest to some of the allegations in family court, he would have Lisa back within two weeks. It had been almost a month.

"This conversation is just between me and you, right?" Smith asked the detective again.

"That's correct, and I have no problem with that. However, I can see there might be a problem with your attorney. He might complain about me taking you out for a soda and talking with you," Dylhoff stated, aware he had not read Smith his Miranda rights.

"Don't worry about that. It was my request and I pay his bills," Smith said arrogantly.

Smith and Dylhoff's "good buddy" conversation lasted two hours. By the time Dylhoff had deposited Smith at the county jail and returned to his office, he was ecstatic at the thought of proving Khris Smith had been murdered by her husband. He immediately contacted Lieutenant Hudeck and advised him that Russ Smith was willing to talk and give them what they needed to connect him directly to the murder, if the department was willing to work with him.

Next Dylhoff contacted Jeff Fink, head prosecutor

at juvenile court, and discussed the options for Lisa that Russ had requested.

The prosecutor told Dylhoff that there were basically three options for placement of Lisa:

1. Smith could release his rights to the Department of Social Services (DSS) and they would do a study and properly place her.
2. There could be a guardianship where Smith would pick who Lisa went to. The home would be studied by DSS and reviewed by the court. If it was found to be acceptable, Lisa would be placed there. That person would complete an annual report to the court on the placement.
3. Smith could pick the placement and Lisa would be placed there on what they call a "direct consent adoption." Again it would involve a home study by the court.

Fink told Dylhoff that any of the options would require scrutiny of the potential home and that could take up to two months, and in the end the family court judge would have the final say as to where Lisa would be placed. The only thing that could speed up the process would be if Smith himself was willing to pay for the home study, the cost running several hundred dollars. Fink assured Dylhoff that the immediate families were first considered for any long-term placements. Fink reiterated that there could be no promises made to Smith at that point in the discussions.

Dylhoff drove back to the KCSD, contemplating Smith's offer and the prosecutor's response. Smith was ready to confess. He appeared weary of carrying the dark secret of where Khris was and what had happened to her. He seemed annoyed at the police investigation and tired of the cat-and-mouse game of surveillance he'd once thought humorous.

As Dylhoff drove along the darkened streets of Kalamazoo to the sheriff's department, he reviewed his strategy. Smith had been a reserve officer. From all indications he had been obsessed by the uniform, the power. Dylhoff had brought Smith to a point of friendly discussion; perhaps it was time to appeal to his powerful ego and draw on the part of his personality that would relish the idea of being "part of the investigation" instead of the focus of it. As soon as Dylhoff reached the KCSD he phoned Smith.

"As a former police officer, you know the laws pertaining to murder, second-degree murder, and manslaughter," Dylhoff stated. "Did you do anything that would be more than manslaughter?"

"No, Randy! You know that as well," Smith declared.

"Leading up to the incident, there is nothing at all that happened that would indicate that there was anything more than manslaughter?" Dylhoff inquired again.

"No," Smith said once more.

"How about after the fact?" Dylhoff questioned.

There was a momentary pause on the other end of the line. "I guess that would be a matter of interpretation," Smith finally replied.

Dylhoff explained to Smith that the time that had lapsed since Khris's disappearance and everything that had been done to cover things up gave the appearance of an event that had been planned.

Smith took a deep breath, audible on the line.

"That was time I was able to spend with Lisa," Smith

said. "I was able to be with her from September until January."

There was another long pause.

"Do you think things would have been different if I told you these things the first time we talked?" Smith asked.

"It wouldn't have looked premeditated. It would probably have given a greater appearance of manslaughter," Dylhoff replied.

Smith disagreed. He didn't think things would have turned out any differently. He rationalized that he wouldn't have found out certain things about Khris, discovered the kind of person she really was.

"There's a whole other side to this incident that needs to be told," Smith stated.

Wanting to keep the momentum going, to sustain Smith's obvious need to release himself from the deadly truth, Dylhoff assured Smith he was the only one who could reveal the truth. All the police had was Smith's side of the story. Khris wasn't there to dispute it.

"My only concern is for Lisa's welfare," Smith reemphasized. "Nothing else means anything to me. She's all I have."

Dylhoff kept the friendly yet edgy conversation going. He needed Smith to keep talking, hoping it would eventually lead him to the truth about Khris. Dylhoff continued to talk about Lisa, the one thing he knew Smith cared about.

"Khris planned everything for Lisa from the time she got up in the morning until the time she went to bed," Smith said, his voice laced with bitterness. "She picked Lisa's friends for her. Everything."

"Isn't it funny," Dylhoff baited Smith, "Khris is gone and she's still creating problems for you."

"Yeah, somewhat, but nothing like it was before," Smith insisted. "Lisa doesn't even miss her and she's doing better now that Khris is gone."

Smith admitted to Dylhoff that he knew what he had done wasn't right and that he knew right from wrong. Smith wanted to be assured that his daughter would be placed with his family and he didn't want to tell her anything until after he had "paid the piper" for what he had done.

"Randy," Smith said as if talking to a longtime friend and confidant, "how do I tell her?"

More than anything, Smith wanted to watch his daughter grow up. To walk her down the aisle when she married. It seemed Smith was suddenly in a rush to expedite things.

"I feel it shouldn't take more than six to eight years, which I'm willing to pay," Smith stated, suggesting the sentence he would accept as punishment for his sinful deed.

It was obvious Smith wanted to be in control. To call the shots. Dylhoff knew the prosecutor wasn't willing to make any promises, but he would continue to let Smith make his demands. It was imperative to get Smith's confession.

Chapter 16

Russ Smith was anxious. He had made his decision to move forward with his confession. All that had to be done to set the wheels in motion was for the prosecutor to agree to the manslaughter charge and for Lisa to be placed with one of his relatives. They seemed like simple requests to Smith. Agree to his terms and the case could be cleared. It would be neat and tidy. No more scrutiny by the police. No more sleepless nights.

Smith couldn't wait any longer for Detective Dylhoff's call. On March 22, 1995, he again phoned Dylhoff's office.

"What have you found out?" Smith asked anxiously.

"I think it's better if we discuss it in person, rather than over the phone," Dylhoff said.

Within two hours Dylhoff was sitting across from Smith at the Kalamazoo County Jail.

"Lieutenant Hudeck, prosecutors Jim Gregart and Robert Pangle, and I met to discuss the case and your requests," Dylhoff began. "Both prosecutors advised they can't make any promises and won't agree to a specific charge of manslaughter without reviewing the facts."

Within seconds Smith's face changed from optimistic to dejected. He had hoped the legal team would accept his offer to tell them the facts in exchange for the lesser plea.

"They advised that they couldn't morally, ethically, or legally agree to manslaughter without the facts in front of them. They need to know what you did before, during, and after the incident," Dylhoff continued. "Russ, they won't promise anything but that they will review the case based upon the facts furnished to them. And it would be reviewed for the appropriate charge."

Smith sat speechless, contemplating what Dylhoff had told him.

"The only difference between manslaughter and second-degree murder is the time element," Dylhoff told Smith. "On the point system they use, the best that you would get would be four to fifteen years on second-degree murder, and the worst would be eight to twenty-five years. On a manslaughter charge the worst would be two to seven years, the best one to five."

"There's no way I'm going down for twenty years," Smith said in a raised voice.

Smith wanted the whole thing to come to a conclusion. No trial. No hassle. If he walked in the prison door that day, he wanted to know when he would be walking out. Smith needed a month to get his finances in order, sell his house, sell his car, and get some things paid off. He wanted to spend a little time with his daughter, to make sure she was in the custody of his parents. If he could do that, Smith said he would have no problem walking through the prison door, but he continued to insist he wouldn't do it if he was going down for twenty years.

"I'll figure out a way to take care of myself before I

allow that to happen," Smith threatened. "I just want this over."

Smith's features turned from harsh to gentle as he again spoke of Lisa and his desire for her to be shielded from the publicity that was sure to be part of his conviction.

"It needs to be over for you, for me, for the family, for the community, and for the press," Dylhoff advised. "But if we can't get an agreement worked out and we charge you through the circumstantial evidence and physical evidence we have, it will be an open murder charge. You can't imagine the publicity that would surround you, even if you were to be found not guilty. On the other hand, if we can work out something and you plea to it, it will only be a news story for a short time."

"Yeah, maybe eight to ten days, then it'd be all over," Smith agreed.

As Dylhoff and Smith continued to talk, Smith's trust in the detective was apparent. Dylhoff only hoped he could get all parties to agree to a reasonable settlement.

By the end of the conversation, Smith had said he would agree to second-degree murder with the lower end of the sentencing charge, if Lisa could be placed with his parents and he would know she would remain there until she was eighteen years old.

As Dylhoff drove back to his office, he felt a sense of accomplishment. Smith had relented on the manslaughter charge. Negotiations were progressing. Dylhoff could sense the successful conclusion of a very difficult case. It made his heart race.

* * *

Upon returning to his office at the Portage PD, Dylhoff sat in the small office he shared with another
detective. As he eyed the clutter of three-ring binders,
faxes, and notepads, his desk phone rang. It was Mark
Charter, attorney for Russ Smith. Charter advised the
police veteran that he didn't want him talking directly
with his client, and he had told Russ Smith the same
thing.

"He contacted me and wanted me to come and talk
with him," Dylhoff said, an air of irritability in his voice.

Charter indicated he had no problem with the detective speaking to Smith, as long as he was also present.
Charter felt out of the loop and he wanted in. Dylhoff
had been spending more time with his client than
Charter had, and the attorney wasn't pleased. Charter
even expressed anger that Dylhoff had taken his client
and "driven all over the county" the previous day.

Dylhoff remained cool. He was experienced in
dealing with attorneys and wasn't going to let Smith's
hired gun intimidate him.

"Russ requested I take him for a soda, and the way
I understand it, if he requested me to come and talk
to him, I can legally do that," Dylhoff replied.

Charter told Dylhoff he didn't care, that he was
telling him he didn't want him talking directly to
his client. Dylhoff then heard the hang-up click of
Charter's phone.

The detective was just beginning to cool down following the confrontation with Charter when Smith
called from the county jail.

"I can't get your bond reduced to ten percent as you
requested," Dylhoff advised, "and your attorney contacted me, telling me not to have any contact with you."

"He's my problem," Smith assured Dylhoff. "I

haven't changed my decision about what I want. I'll call you back tomorrow."

Dylhoff replaced the receiver in the cradle and stared out the window. Although the winter snows were gone, from the condensation that shrouded the glass, it was clearly cold outside. Charter could make his negotiations with Smith difficult, if not impossible. Dylhoff, like Smith, was anxious to get Smith's admission of guilt on the record and the Smith case off the books. Dylhoff knew he was close, but he also knew that until the ink was dry on the plea agreement, anything could happen.

The investigation of Khris Smith's mysterious disappearance and possible murder would continue until an indictment was entered. Dylhoff and other investigators continued to follow leads as they would in any other inquiry.

A certificate of analysis was received from Roche Laboratories concerning samples taken from the fillet knife and the bed of Smith's pickup truck. The report indicated there had been no DNA detected on the knife and no human DNA detected on the two samples out of the truck. As with the garage carpet, the knife and truck bed had been a dead end.

As promised, Russ Smith called to check on the progress of his requests. Dylhoff informed Smith that there was going to be no bond reduction in regard to his embezzlement case and no guarantees from the prosecutor's office for the case concerning Khris.

Fifteen minutes after the phone call from Smith, Dylhoff and Detective Palenick were at the jail to talk with Smith face-to-face.

"Since your attorney has contacted me," Dylhoff began, "I need to advise you of your right to have an attorney present during this interview. Do you want your attorney here?"

"I'm not sure," Smith replied.

Dylhoff informed Smith that since there was a possibility that an attorney was involved in the case, he would first have to determine if he was willing to waive his right to counsel being present during questioning before they could talk.

"Does that mean I don't have to answer anything?" Smith asked.

"That's right."

"Well, go ahead and read me my Miranda rights," Smith instructed.

"You have the right to remain silent," Dylhoff began, ending by asking Smith if he understood those rights.

"Yes," Smith replied.

Smith was willing to talk with Dylhoff and Palenick but indicated that it would most likely be a one-sided conversation, with the detectives giving all the information.

"If there's a point where I say 'no,' or 'that's enough,' am I entitled to that?" Smith questioned.

The detectives assured Smith he had the right to stop the interview at any point and refuse to talk without his attorney present.

Charter had actually been retained to represent Smith in both his divorce action against Khris and his embezzlement charge by Sears. He had not been officially retained to represent Smith in the case involving Khris's disappearance and possible death, but the attorney had been proactive in looking out for his client's best interest in all proceedings.

Smith appeared to relax somewhat. He listened carefully as Dylhoff explained that the family court had begun the process of doing a home study for an out-of-state placement of Lisa with his parents. Again no promises were made except that the investigation of Khris Smith's disappearance would continue, with or without Smith's assistance.

Chapter 17

On March 16, 1995, Russell Smith sat down and wrote two letters to Don Sewell, the main Sears store manager. Smith knew the time was fast approaching that he would be arrested and charged with embezzlement. The first letter was a standard resignation statement.

Don,

Please accept this letter as my resignation of employment at Sears Roebuck and Co. I feel that it is in the best interest of all parties involved. That at this time I persue (*sic*) employment interests outside of Sears.

Sincerely,
Russell Smith

Smith's second letter was more personal.

Don,

I will be out of town for the next few days. I don't kow if there is anything else that you need to get from me. I'll call you when I get back.

You have been "without a doubt" the best

store mgr. that I ever had the pleasure of working with.

Thanks,
Russ

P.S. Can you answer questions about profit
sharing, pension, accrued vacation, etc.?

Within days of writing the letters to Sewell, Russ
Smith was arrested.

Lisa Smith was angry. She had read the newspaper
article in the *Gazette*'s Sunday edition concerning her
father's indictment for embezzlement. She was upset
with him and didn't want to see him. Most of the
child's anger was because both her parents had with-
held information from her. She hadn't known her
mother was four months pregnant with her before
her parents married, nor did she know that her daddy
had been married before. Lisa felt betrayed.

On March 24, 1995, shortly after Russ Smith bonded
out of jail, he called Lisa's foster mother requesting a
visit. As always, she advised Smith he would have to go
through Protective Services.

"I'm aware of that," Smith said angrily. "But I haven't
seen my daughter in a week. I want to talk to her and I
want to see her." Smith needed to make certain his
daughter knew she had nothing to do with his arrest.
But a visit with Lisa wasn't going to happen as soon as
he would have liked.

"You can't," the foster mother responded, and
hung up the phone.

Smith had told Dylhoff during their discussion that

he wanted, needed, to talk to Lisa before he went any further in their negotiations for his admission of guilt. Now that he was released from jail, he had a burn to see Lisa, a necessity to explain his actions.

Leads continued to flow into the Portage Police Department regarding the disappearance of Khris Smith. Although a man named Rick Blake had called weeks earlier and left a message that he had information pertaining to Khris—with so many leads to follow, people to interview, and discussions between the prosecutor and Smith concerning an appropriate charge—Detective Dylhoff didn't contact Blake until March 28, 1995.

Twenty-five-year-old Rick Blake had been employed by Advance Pool and Spa during the summer of 1993. While he was working in the retail area, an attractive brunette, wearing tight-fitting blue jeans and a tank top, had strolled in. She had a young girl with her.

Khris Smith introduced herself to Blake and told him she had recently moved into the area from Indiana.

"There have been some lawn workers and construction workers around and they've ground dirt and other materials into the cement on the driveway," Khris had explained. "I want to clean them off with muriatic acid."

Khris knew that muriatic acid was a liquid compound often found at pool supplies for breaking down algae on the surface of gunite pools. She had hoped the blend would rid her of the unsightly stains on the driveway of her new home.

Blake made the sale and carried the acid to Khris's car, carefully placing it in the truck so that it wouldn't spill and damage the trunk's interior. Blake thought

Khris polite and attractive, but he gave little thought to her once she pulled away from the store. Ten minutes later the office phone rang.

The caller identified herself as Khris Smith. She reminded him that she had just been in to purchase muriatic acid, then asked Blake his age.

"I like the way you carry yourself. Your posture," Khris said. "Are you married?"

When Blake responded no, Khris told him she was.

"Why did you call?" Blake asked.

"I'm new in the area and don't know a lot of people. I liked the way you carried yourself. You seem like a very nice guy," Khris responded.

"If you're married, why are you so interested in talking with me?" Blake inquired.

Khris indicated she wasn't happy in her marriage and that the only reason she was sticking around was for the sake of her daughter. "I feel a daughter should be raised with both a father and a mother figure," Khris stated. "That's the only reason why I'm in the relationship."

Blake sensed Khris wanted some kind of physical relationship with him, but he wasn't interested in sneaking around with a married woman. There was more trouble there than he needed and he told Khris Smith exactly that.

Khris voiced her disappointment and told Blake that perhaps they could just meet for a drink sometime.

"Yeah, maybe sometime we'll run into each other again," Blake said offhandedly, knowing there was no way he would be meeting this or any other married woman for drinks. If Khris hadn't been married, perhaps Blake would have taken her up on the offer, but he was steadfast in his refusal.

After explaining his encounter with Khris Smith to Detective Dylhoff, Blake stated that when he first began seeing articles in the paper concerning her disappearance, and the picture of Khris, he knew without a doubt it was the same woman who had flirted with him at the pool store.

Dylhoff took notes as Blake spoke. Was Khris Smith so unhappy that she would have left Russ and taken Lisa with her? If she'd threatened to run off, it could be the motive for murder they were looking for.

An interview with Kevin Pennington, a Smith coworker, basically gave Dylhoff the same impression of the Smith marriage. Pennington talked of how Smith seldom mentioned Khris but would talk continuously about Lisa. When the two men would go on a trip, Khris would call Russ every night. Russ would speak only briefly to his wife, while spending extended time talking with his daughter. "He basically tucked her in bed over the phone," Pennington told Dylhoff.

Pennington also revealed that on more than one occasion he had seen Smith's car at the residence of a female at the Spring Lake Apartment Complex between 3:30 and 4:00 A.M. These late-night/early-morning visits took place prior to Khris's disappearance.

Rick Blake and Kevin Pennington's declarations, together with numerous statements from Smith's Sears coworkers, formed a picture of a couple in crisis. Dylhoff was certain Smith had killed Khris; after all, Smith had even implicated himself during their discussions. But because Smith wasn't getting the cooperation he desired from the prosecutor's office, it was now Dylhoff's challenge to move forward. He had to come up with a solid motive and better yet . . . a body.

Chapter 18

Sergeant John Kenney with the Michigan State Police Aviation Division arrived at the Kalamazoo Airport at 11:00 A.M. on April 6, 1995, six months after Khris Smith's disappearance. Detective Dylhoff had contacted Kenney to aid in an aerial infrared search of local wooded areas, as well as to conduct visual flyovers of area lakes. The search had been set for April 4, but due to windy conditions, the flight had been delayed two days.

As Detectives Randy Dylhoff and Ron Petroski approached the MSP helicopter, they ducked to protect their heads from the swirling blades before climbing aboard the craft piloted by Kenney. The Atwater Pond near Twelfth Street and Milham, as well as the wooded area near Kalamazoo Valley Community College, netted nothing out of the ordinary. A barrel in the shallow portion of Sugarloaf Lake off Shaver Road was spotted, but it proved to be nothing more than rubbish. A visual of Gull Lake showed nothing unusual in the water. Although a lot of the shoreline was visible, near the center of the lake where the water was obviously deep, visibility was severely limited.

Kenney's participation in the aerial search was helpful, even though it didn't result in finding Khris Smith's body. The scan told Dylhoff and Petroski that *if* Russ Smith had disposed of his wife's body in Gull Lake, it would be found in the depths of the dark waters in the center of the vast body of water.

Following Smith's March 22, 1995, indictment for embezzlement and the newspaper stories that followed, more women who had dated Russ Smith began to contact Dylhoff at the Portage PD. Their stories were not unlike that told by Raquel Owens.

Thirty-six-year-old Lori Hawkins had seen the ad in the *Kalamazoo Gazette* in mid-December. It had appeared in the Datelines section under the heading "Quixotic."

"QUIXOTIC"

I'm 32 years old, 6'1", 175 lbs. I enjoy most outdoor activities as well as quiet times at home. ISO attractive female for adventurous friendship. Kalamazoo area, code 3587.

The word "quixotic" caught Lori's eye, even though she had to look up the meaning in the dictionary. The definition intrigued her even more: "Quixotic: Idealistic to an impractical degree; marked by lofty romantic ideas on extravagantly chivalrous action."

It had sounded like the kind of man Lori would be interested in meeting. She called Smith. They agreed to meet at Chili's for a drink after her regularly scheduled Wednesday-night soccer game.

Lori Hawkins, five foot five and athletic, was impressed with the tall, well-built, handsome man she had spoken to only by phone. Over drinks Smith said he had been a single parent for about three months. He explained to Lori that after his wife abandoned him and his daughter, he had sought psychiatric counseling. He claimed he had been advised to "get a life," so he put an ad in the newspaper and had been having a good time ever since. Smith made it clear he wasn't into the bar scene, opting instead for the personal ads. He claimed Lori was the second or third person who had called him after reading the ad.

Smith spoke of his daughter, even telling Lori about Lisa's request to have her hair dyed and the disastrous results.

Lori liked Smith. To her, he seemed very calm, cool, and collected. He was very nice. She agreed to a second date, lunch at Applebee's on West Main several weeks later. Again Smith appeared mannerly and levelheaded.

On New Year's weekend Smith went to Lori's residence, taking Lisa with him. They ordered pizza and watched the Orange Bowl game on TV. Lisa was a polite child, but Lori thought that her mannerisms and speech made her appear to be a kid who was seven years old, going on seventeen.

Hawkins told Dylhoff that she had been out of town on a business trip when the news of Khris Smith's disappearance hit the papers. She hadn't personally seen the articles but had been told about them by a friend. After hearing the news that Smith's wife had vanished, Lori made no contact with Smith. With all the speculation of his involvement in Khris's mysterious departure, and everything she was being told by friends about Smith, Hawkins had no desire to reconnect with him.

Dylhoff made notes regarding his conversation with

Lori Hawkins. The information garnered gave Dyl-hoff no new insight into the whereabouts of Khris Smith or of Russ Smith's direct involvement in her disappearance. Lori's story, much like that told to him by Raquel Owens, depicted Smith as a man who knew for certain his wife would not be returning.

Catherine Singleton had frequently dated Russell Smith and the two had apparently become good friends. Catherine met Smith through an ad she her-self had placed in the weekly newspaper *Flashes* personals. Smith had contacted her early in Janu-ary 1995, just about four months after his wife's disappearance.

Catherine also found Russ Smith to be charming. He'd bring her a rose each time he saw her. Some-thing he may have learned when he read *A Rose for Her Grave*. Smith indicated he was a daring person, looking for adventure.

"How adventurous a person are you?" Smith had asked as they sat by the fireplace at Smith's house, drinking wine and listening to music. Catherine was uncertain how to answer Smith's question, which could have a number of connotations. She avoided answering by asking about his house. As with the other women, Smith gave Catherine a limited tour of his home, restricting her access to the main floor.

Smith told Singleton that his wife had left him and taken their daughter with her. He talked often of Lisa and his love for her.

Smith had been at Catherine's house for dinner but was nervous and tense because several additional people he didn't know had been in the house. When

Catherine commented she had seen the news of his arrest for embezzlement and asked Smith about the charges at Sears, Smith had simply stated that "stuff" had started piling up; he didn't like clutter, so he started selling it cheap. He even admitted he sold himself a $1,200 snowblower for $200.

Singleton admitted she had pursued Smith, hoping for an in-depth, stable relationship, but Smith indicated he wasn't interested in anything long-term. She hadn't seen him since the Sunday following his release from jail. Smith apparently had become frustrated with women, in general, and Khris, in particular. When Catherine spoke with Detective Dylhoff about her relationship with Smith, she said, "He told me women are more of a bother than they're worth and that the only female he was concerned about that was worth anything was his daughter. No woman would come before Lisa. He said the first time he got married, it was for lust, the second time was definitely for love, and that if he was ever to get married again, it would be for money."

According to Catherine Singleton, Smith had been slipping into the depths of despair. He confided in her that he hadn't cried since Lisa was taken from him, and he was afraid that if he started, he wouldn't be able to stop. Smith had even revealed there had been times when he thought of going really fast in the Mustang he called "arrest me red" and slamming it into a tree.

During the short time they dated, Smith displayed symptoms of paranoia along with intermittent bouts of depression. He talked to Catherine about the cops following him, hoping he would lead them to evidence. Smith, though, claimed there was none to be found. He appeared to consider his shadowing by the police a big game, a joke. More than likely, the narcissistic side of Smith believed he had committed the perfect crime.

"But he'll slip up," Singleton explained. "He likes his wine and when the wine flows, so does his mouth."

Catherine felt no sympathy for Smith, only contempt.

"He's lied to me and he's been deceptive about his relationships with other women," Catherine Singleton told Dylhoff. "He is only out for himself. He is actually an arrogant, pompous ass."

The fourth in a series of women whom Dylhoff talked to was Lynda Banister, a thirty-six-year-old living in Portage. Although Lynda had only dated Smith a couple of times, the information she gave Dylhoff helped assure the detective that he was on the right track.

"I inquired if his ex-wife lived nearby so he could see his daughter frequently," Lynda said. "He stated yes, she was in Gull Lake."

Lynda hadn't thought much about it, assuming Smith meant his wife lived in the Gull Lake area. Dylhoff, however, believed that Smith was playing a word game with her. Dylhoff was certain Khris Smith's body lay somewhere beneath the deep, cold waters of Gull Lake.

Dylhoff had been spending so much time running down leads on the Khris Smith disappearance that he hadn't checked on Lisa for several weeks. He decided it was time to make contact with Lisa's foster mother.

"How are things going with Lisa?" Dylhoff asked when he had Teresa on the phone.

"Things had been going fairly well. However, the last couple of weeks she has been off her afternoon Ritalin medication. She's been waking up during the night crying, apparently having nightmares," Teresa said. "When she wakes up, she is crying and yelling, 'Don't hurt my mommy. Leave my mommy alone.' I go in to comfort her, to see if she wants to talk about what she's thinking. She told me, 'I'm not going to talk about it. I need to protect my dad.'"

Dylhoff, who had been leaning back in his chair, sat up straight. "Did she say anything else?" he asked anxiously.

"She asked if we could adopt her and raise her forever and ever. When I asked why, she said, 'My mom's dead. My dad's going to hell. Where am I going to go?'"

Dylhoff could hear the distress in Teresa's voice. She cared about the foster children who had come in and gone out of her home over the years. In fact, Teresa and her husband were in the process of adopting one of the boys they had once taken in on a temporary basis.

"Lisa has made comments and appears to realize that she is not going to see her mommy again and that she's dead. I've asked her several times why she feels that way, but she closes up and doesn't want to talk about it. I haven't pushed the issue," Teresa stated.

Dylhoff felt secure that Lisa was in good hands . . . for the time being.

A week later, Dylhoff was contacted by Tim Orosz. Smith's neighbor on Thunderbay had been visited by Khris Smith's mother and brother, Kay and Troy Klein. The Kleins were passing through town on their way back to Florida after spending the previous week in Ohio for Kay's mother's funeral.

Dylhoff was anxious to know if Khris had shown up for her grandmother's burial. The two had shared an especially close relationship. But according to Orosz, Kay stated Khris hadn't been in attendance.

Kay and Troy were in Portage to see Lisa and had been granted a supervised visit at the McDonald's on Sprinkle Road. Kay had requested that Tim and Debbie bring their children to McDonald's so the three children could play.

Tim told Dylhoff that although they didn't talk with Kay at length about the case, she had indicated that she was upset with the police department, believing they were dragging their feet. Evidently, Kay had hired an attorney and had also written letters to various senators and congressmen in an attempt to get answers to her questions. Dylhoff's eyes rolled at the news.

Kay Klein wasn't the only one who wanted answers to her daughter's disappearance. The department was following every lead, checking and rechecking with insurance companies, health care providers, family and friends, in an effort to find out if Khris Smith had contacted anyone over the past nine months. Smith had even been close to a full confession.

After hanging up with Tim Orosz, Dylhoff leafed through his notes. With all the information obtained to date, Dylhoff believed the investigation should be officially changed from a missing person to a homicide.

Chapter 19

Julie Moore met Russ Smith while at the Brown Derby Restaurant with her best friend, Rebecca Dodd. Rebecca couldn't recall why she had seen Smith in the newspaper, but her intuition told her he was not someone she wanted her best friend spending time with. Rebecca had even warned Julie that getting close to Smith wouldn't be a good idea.

Julie assured her friend that her relationship with Smith was only short-term. She enjoyed their time together and she intended to continue seeing him. The temporary kinship between Russ Smith and Julie Moore turned into weeks of steady dating, culminating with Julie's moving into the house Russ had shared with his wife and daughter.

Lisa Smith didn't like Julie Moore. Following a day-long visit with her father and grandparents, watching her father and this new woman together, she told her foster mother that she disliked Julie because she was "always kissing my daddy."

Lisa probably wouldn't have liked anyone who was taking her mother's place in her father's house, and especially in her father's heart. What had made the visit more stressful for the young girl was that it was over Mother's Day weekend, a special time she had always enjoyed sharing with Khris. This was a time she missed her mother more than ever.

Lisa felt more than simple jealousy over Julie Moore. When Lisa returned to the foster home after spending the weekend with her father, grandparents, and Julie, she was distressed and anxious.

"I know my mommy is dead," Lisa told her foster mother. "And I think my daddy had something to do with her going away."

Teresa's heart went out to the small child she held in her arms. She wished she could do more to comfort her, to help her through the nightmare she had been living for nearly eight months. But the pressure of caring for Lisa, dealing with Russ Smith, and awaiting the court's decision as to where Lisa would be placed was taking a toll on Teresa's own health. Since Lisa had been in her home, Teresa's blood pressure had continuously gone up and was higher than her physician thought safe. Lisa was going to have to be transferred to another foster home as soon as school was out. Lisa Smith would be losing a mother figure for the second time in less than a year.

In early June, Detective Dylhoff returned to the Mermaid Lounge to talk with a dancer known as "Cinnamon." The Latin stripper remembered Russ Smith well.

"The first night I worked, Russ Smith and his friend Bob Kilgore came into the club. Both of them tipped quite heavily. Russ tipped me a total of one hundred and forty dollars over the course of the night, all in twenty-dollar bills," Cinnamon told the detective. But the next time they came in, and since then, Smith only tipped her with one-dollar bills, and at the most he only spent a total of forty dollars in an evening.

Cinnamon mentioned that Smith, dressed in a suit and tie the first night she had seen him, had given the illusion of a wealthy businessman. The way he tipped, she was certain he was well-to-do. But on his third visit to the Mermaid Lounge, Smith had given her his Sears business card. Noticing that he was in the automotive center, she couldn't understand how he could spend more than a hundred dollars tipping her, considering the wages he earned at Sears.

Noticing that Smith's ring finger bore the indentation of a ring, she had asked him if he was married. He said, "No, I've never been married," Cinnamon told Dylhoff.

Smith had asked Cinnamon out a couple of times. She had declined. She did, however, give him her home phone number and he had called several times. Smith had left some strange messages about her not going out with him and standing him up. It had made the stripper uneasy enough to change her phone number and not give it to Smith again.

"I heard that Russ has a new girlfriend and is even possibly talking marriage," Cinnamon told the detective. "I haven't seen Russ or Bob in quite a while; then yesterday they come in the club."

From Cinnamon's explanation, Smith had evidently told Julie Moore that he and Bob had gone to play golf, but they were at the Mermaid Lounge instead.

"Bob told me Russ is really smart," Cinnamon said. "He told me Russ had been a cop before he came here. He said Russ is smarter than the cops give him credit for. He talked about how if Khris was dumped in a lake, that there are so many lakes that she would never be found."

As Dylhoff took notes, he hesitated, his pen poised over his notebook. According to Cinnamon, Smith had made yet another reference to Khris Smith possibly being in one of the many lakes that surrounded Kalamazoo County.

"He also made a comment about a cemetery and that nobody looks twice in a cemetery where people are buried," Cinnamon said, interrupting Dylhoff's thoughts. "One of the last comments Bob made was that if Russ did do it, the cops will never find the body."

Dylhoff begged to differ.

On June 5, 1995, almost nine months into the investigation of Khris Smith's disappearance, Dylhoff arranged to meet with Julie Moore at the Celery Flats Park pavilion, in Portage.

While sitting under the pavilion canopy, protected from the summer sun, Julie told the detective about meeting Russ Smith on March 31, 1995, at the Brown Derby in Kalamazoo. Her first impression of him was that he was the "playboy type." His gold necklaces, bracelets, and earring were not her style. When she told him she didn't care for all the gold bangles, he had immediately stopped wearing them, showing Julie a kind and considerate side. He was gentle and loving toward her nine-year-old son as well as to her. He never showed signs of anger or meanness.

"I'm in love with him," Moore admitted, "even knowing a little bit about his past."

Dylhoff's expression didn't change. He gave no indication of the fear he had for anyone who got close to Russ Smith, adult or child.

A cool breeze blew Julie's hair as she spoke. "All I know is what I've read in the newspaper. Russ has kept all the newspaper articles and has let me read them. I think the articles have been very slanted against Russ. I believe there is nothing, and that there has been nothing going on between Russ and Lisa. He loves his daughter more dearly than anything."

Julie Moore was in denial. Like so many women who refuse to believe a husband or boyfriend has sexually abused their child in fear of losing the man they love, Julie Moore chose to be blindfolded by her emotions.

"Have you talked with Russ about the disappearance of Khristine?" Dylhoff asked.

"If you don't want to know the answer, you don't ask the question," Moore replied faintly. "I know I'll have to ask him about his involvement eventually. I don't know what my future with him holds, but at this point in my life, I feel very close to him. I enjoy his companionship. I feel our relationship should continue."

Julie seemed saddened by the thought of losing Russ Smith. She talked about Smith advising her that it would probably be best to cut their relationship off because of the publicity surrounding the accusations against him. But Julie was in love and she liked the way that made her feel.

As wonderful as Julie Moore believed Russ Smith to be, her ex-husband, Dennis, believed him to be evil. The long-distance truck driver had heard about the disappearance of Smith's wife, along with the allegations of Smith being involved with his daughter. He was concerned for the welfare and safety of his son.

Because Julie didn't see Russ Smith as a problem

and expressed no fear for her safety or the safety of
their son, Dennis Moore decided to get some type of
restraining order. He had to do all he could to keep
Smith away from his boy.

When Dennis Moore told Detective Dylhoff of his
misgivings about Smith, he related a conversation he
had with Julie a short time before meeting with the
detective.

"I point-blank told her that Russ killed his wife,"
Dennis stated. "Julie's response was 'What if it was an
accident?' To which I asked her, 'Did he tell you that?'
She said, 'No, I'm talking hypothetically.'"

As Dennis and Julie Moore continued to discuss
Smith and his missing wife, Julie stated that Khris
Smith was really a rotten person. "You know nothing
about his ex-wife," Julie told Dennis. "She was a
whore." In reality, Julie didn't know Khris Smith either, only what she was told by Russ.

Dennis Moore knew there was nothing he could do
to change Julie's mind about the man she had become emotionally involved with. All he could do was
protect his son in any way he could.

Though the Department of Social Services had tried,
they were unable to find a foster home for Lisa. She
would have to be moved to either the Juvenile Home or
Lakeside Girl's Home, if she could no longer stay with
Teresa and her family. The Ohio and Florida home
studies were dragging on longer than expected.

Rather than see Lisa go to a group home of any
kind, Teresa decided it would be okay for Lisa to stay
with her. But Teresa was planning on leaving for the
weekend, and approval of the judge would have to be

obtained for Lisa to go with her on the out-of-state excursion.

Permission was given, and from Saturday to Wednesday, Lisa accompanied her foster family to Olney, Illinois, to visit their relatives. The DSS had been unable to reach Russ Smith in person to advise him of the unexpected trip, but a message was left on his answering machine.

During their trip Teresa had encouraged Lisa to telephone her father.

"Do I have to?" Lisa responded.

"No, you don't *have* to," Teresa said.

"Well, then I won't," Lisa stated flatly.

Beginning the Friday of their return, Teresa began to receive hang-up phone calls. There had been eight from Friday evening until Sunday. Whoever was calling was blocking Teresa's caller ID. She had no way of knowing for certain who the caller was, but she suspected it was Russ Smith.

After speaking with Teresa, Dylhoff decided it was time to have Detective Michelle Wright interview Lisa. The department had been treading lightly with the child, but pointed questions needed to be asked— and answered.

Detective Wright arrived at Teresa's home on June 15, 1995, at 11:30 A.M. Lisa Smith hadn't seen or heard from her mother in almost nine months. The attractive female detective began slowly, letting the eight-year-old girl know that all she wanted was for her to be honest.

"You don't have to talk about anything you don't feel comfortable with, and if I ask a question you don't like, all you have to do is tell me you don't want to talk," Wright said calmly.

Wright started out reviewing activities Lisa had

been involved in, including dance, piano, and soccer. The child was quick to point out that she hadn't played soccer, which indicated to Wright that Lisa was comfortable pointing out the detective's mistake.

Lisa indicated that at times her mom and dad argued and yelled at each other, occasionally keeping her awake at night. She stated that they sometimes even pushed each other, which frightened her.

"I was afraid they'd knock each other down," Lisa said, "but that never happened. I remember two times when they were pushing each other—once in the kitchen and the other time in the living room."

"Did your dad ever hit you?" Wright asked softly.

"Not with his fists, but he hit me with a yardstick," Lisa said as tears dampened her eyes and her voice fluctuated. "It left bruises on my bottom and it hurt when I sat down for several days."

Wright could tell from Lisa's physical reaction to this discussion of being hit with the yardstick that it had not only been a painful experience at the time, but one she continued to carry with her.

Lisa seemed to be frustrated that she had been instructed by her father not to discuss her mother's disappearance with her friends. Her father wouldn't talk to her about her missing mother either, leaving the child with no one to hear her fears, regrets, and sorrows.

"What do you remember about the day your mother came up missing?" Wright asked.

"Mommy and Daddy weren't arguing, yelling, screaming, or pushing that morning before school. When I got home, my dad told me not to use my bathroom, the one I shared with Mommy. I didn't know why and I was curious. I was able to get the hidden key and go into the bathroom.

"When I got inside, it was all broken up. There were large holes in the wall and the towel rack that usually had towels on it was missing. There weren't any towels in the bathroom, but they had been there before I went to school. The rug on the floor was also gone.

"The shower was broken and the showerhead and drain were missing. The walls looked funny. Daddy told me later he had sanded them."

"Was anything, like shampoo, spilled on the floor?" Wright asked.

"No, and there wasn't any blood in the bathroom," Lisa responded.

Wright stopped momentarily and looked hard at Lisa. She hadn't asked about blood; why would Lisa bring it up?

"Do you know what happened to the rug that was on the floor?" Wright inquired.

"Yes, it was downstairs hanging where Mommy hung wet clothes. It had been washed and was still wet. The washing machine was also going. I think it was towels," Lisa said without stating why she thought towels had been in the washer.

Lisa told Wright that her father had become angry with her for looking in the bathroom. She had then packed some clothes and had gotten into her father's truck to go to her grandparents' house in Ohio. She recalled seeing a barrel in the back of the truck and stated that it held her mother's clothes. Her father said he was taking them to her. She hadn't looked inside the barrel herself.

Detective Wright talked with Lisa about good touches and bad touches.

"A bad touch is something that hurts, and someone leaving you without ever saying good-bye is a bad hurt," Lisa said as tears began to roll down her soft cheeks.

"Lisa, I'm sure your mother leaving hurt a lot, but I think your mother loved you very much," Wright said with sincerity.

"I think my daddy must have hurt Mommy real bad and that's the reason she couldn't come back," Lisa said as the tears stung her eyes. "I think Mommy might be dead."

Chapter 20

Michael Price was the store manager at PicWay Shoes when he first met Khris Smith. Detective Dylhoff wanted to meet with Price to check out a hunch.

Price informed the detective he and Khris became close, although not intimate, during their relationship. She had confided in Price her unhappiness with her marriage and her desire to get out. Neither Price, who was single at the time, nor Khris wanted to have an affair. If they were to be together, it would be when Khris was free from her husband. Khris, however, was afraid, unsure of her ability to care for herself and Lisa. Divorcing, even separating, was a major step Khris Smith was uncertain she was ready to take. But over time she gained confidence, bought her own car, and made plans to take Price up on his offer to take her and her daughter into his life.

Dylhoff pulled from his pocket the three-page letter Russ Smith claimed Khris had left on September 28, 1994. He handed Price the letter and asked him to review it.

Price's eyes roamed over the familiar handwriting.

"Those are some of the thoughts and conversations I had with Khris," Price stated. "I would have been the other man mentioned on the second page of the letter."

If Price were the "other man" in Khris Smith's letter, it had to have been written years before, not the
day of her disappearance.

Price described Khris as a woman who was looking
for a one-man relationship, not someone who would
have a different man everywhere to meet her needs.
Price saw Khris as a person starving for personal, emotional, and psychological affection, not sexual intimacy.
Price claimed Khris just needed a good friend and com-
panion to meet those needs not being met by Russ.

Like Khris Smith's other friends and relatives, Price
couldn't imagine Khris leaving without taking Lisa
with her. When she had talked of leaving with him,
Lisa had definitely been part of that plan.

"She had even talked about how she would fight for
custody of Lisa and do whatever she had to do to keep
her daughter when she left Russ," Price said. "The way
Khristine talked, Russ was a very jealous-type guy."

While Detective Dylhoff was in Ohio visiting with
Michael Price, Lisa Smith was in the same state with
her grandparents and her father for a weeklong vacation. Upon Dylhoff's return, Lisa's foster mother
called.

It seemed that since Lisa's return to Portage, the
child had been on an emotional roller coaster. Tears
accompanied by whimpering had become the norm.

"One evening while running errands with Lisa, I
told her I was getting tired of her whining and crying.
I told her if she needed to yell, scream, or whatever,
to just do it and get it out of her system," Teresa told
Dylhoff. "She said there was nothing bothering her
that she needed to talk about, so she would just have
to keep on crying and whining."

From Teresa's account, Russ and Lisa had come

back to Portage and spent two nights at the house on Thunderbay. Russ slept upstairs and Lisa and her grandparents slept downstairs.

"She then said she wanted to stay with her grandparents in Ohio but that they wouldn't keep her father away from her. She stated, 'Daddy made Mommy go away.' I asked her if she thought that if her mommy left on her own if she would go this long without having any contact with her, to which Lisa stated, 'No, Mommy would have called.' She then said, 'I think my daddy killed my mommy.'"

Teresa described the tears that had run down Lisa's cheeks as she talked about her mother and father.

"I asked her why she thought her daddy did it, and she stated, 'When I went to the bathroom, the day that Mommy left, I saw blood in the sink. My daddy doesn't want me to talk about that and he gets mad when I talk about it. He gets mad when I talk about Mommy.'

"Lisa said she wanted to talk to you, her court-appointed guardian, and the judge. She has a great fear of her dad and what he might do to her."

Three days after talking with Teresa, Dylhoff drove to the now familiar dwelling of Teresa and her family.

As before, Lisa told the detective about the bathtub/shower doors being gone, as well as the rug on the floor in front of the tub. But this time she remembered seeing blood in the bottom of the sink. She stated it was not a lot, but it was enough that she noticed it and knew for sure that it was blood.

Lisa told Dylhoff that while in the house on Thunderbay her father slept upstairs while her grandpa slept in the recliner, her grandmother on one of the couches, and she on the other.

"Daddy told me I could sleep anywhere I wanted. I

told him I wanted to sleep in the living room with Grandpa and Grandma. I knew I would be safe there," Lisa said.

"What do you mean by 'safe'?" Dylhoff asked.

"So that Daddy wouldn't hurt me," Lisa replied.

"How would he hurt you?"

"He would spank me with the paddle. I hate that paddle. I wish I could just throw it away," Lisa said, anger expressed on her face. Dylhoff had read reports indicating that Lisa had suffered bruising on occasion from the paddlings by her father.

"Why didn't you sleep in your room?" Dylhoff questioned.

"I was afraid and didn't want to be upstairs alone with Daddy. Daddy didn't stay Sunday night because he left with Julie," Lisa explained.

"Are there more things you are afraid of with your daddy than just the paddle?" Dylhoff coaxed.

Lisa nodded, her eyes downcast. "I think my daddy killed my mommy."

"Why do you think that?" Dylhoff asked softly.

"Daddy was very angry at me when I went into the bathroom, when he told me not to. There was also no way that Mommy could kick those big holes in the wall in the bathroom."

From the blood Lisa found in the sink, she believed her father had killed her mother. Lisa struggled not to cry during her conversation with Dylhoff, but she was unable to control the tears that fell from her eyes.

"I wanted to live with Grandpa and Grandma, but if they aren't going to keep me safe, then I don't want to live with them," Lisa said.

"What do you mean by keeping you safe?"

"Keeping Daddy away from me."

Dylhoff hoped he would be able to keep Lisa safe, as well as anyone else who became close to Russ Smith, by putting Smith in prison for a very long time. The circumstantial case was good, but without a witness or Smith's confession, there wasn't enough evidence to prosecute. Dylhoff's failure to read Smith his Miranda rights during their "casual conversation" on the way to the Kalamazoo County Jail six weeks before would forever haunt him.

Dylhoff had heard that Russ Smith had sold his home on Thunderbay and moved. He hoped Lisa could tell him more.

"Has your daddy moved yet?" Dylhoff asked.

"Yes. They moved this weekend. All my things are in storage. Daddy said he's staying with Bob Kilgore," Lisa said, referring to Smith's friend and coworker.

Dylhoff, like Teresa, encouraged Lisa to talk with someone about what was going on inside of her. His soft, gentle manner caused tears to again fill Lisa's eyes. She agreed, requesting to speak to one of the counselors suggested by Dylhoff.

"It's important to tell the truth and be open about things that are going on," Dylhoff advised as he squeezed the small child's hand.

Bob Kilgore confirmed that after selling his house for $131,000, Russ Smith had moved in with him. Smith's stay at Kilgore's was short-lived. In less than two weeks, Smith had moved in with Julie Moore and her nine-year-old son. He had stored most of his household goods, as well as Khris's car, at Kuiper Storage on Shaver Road.

Kilgore and Smith remained good friends. On weekends, when Julie wasn't working the concessions at Wings Stadium and Smith wasn't selling spas part-time at L.A. Spas, Kilgore, Moore, and Smith would hang out. On occasion the men had rented a pontoon boat and the three friends had done some fishing on Gull Lake. They had also gone to Traverse City for a weekend and to the Kalamazoo Wine Festival, where they enjoyed wine tasting, live music, and art displays. Smith also appeared to be close to Julie Moore's son, having bought him a $300 gas-powered remote-control car for his birthday.

Although Smith seemed to be enjoying his new life, according to Kilgore, Russ feared he would be going to jail. He was scared most of all of the possibility of not seeing Lisa until she was seventeen years old.

Smith also had a new job as an air conditioner technician for Firestone. Making $8 or $9 an hour as a tech was a considerable step down from his position as a Sears auto manager. But Smith seemed to enjoy many of the same rights and privileges he had as a manager, arriving late and leaving early, making calls and receiving them throughout the day. Julie was a frequent visitor as well, dropping in on Smith two or three times a day, several times a week. They usually left for lunch together each day.

Most of his coworkers at Firestone didn't appreciate the obvious preferential treatment Smith received. One coworker once commented, "He doesn't care about anyone but himself." Coworkers characterized Smith as arrogant, a perfectionist, and a neat freak.

At the end of each day, Smith had his tools cleaned so that they looked brand-new. They were organized in perfect order. His coworkers had to admit he was a good mechanic, insisting that each job be done just right. But what appeared to be an obsessive-compulsive disorder went beyond the job. He washed the red

Mustang frequently, even removing the rims and wheels to clean inside the wheel wells.

The men in the shop knew about Smith's legal problems and marveled at how Smith could give the appearance of having everything under control. "He acts like he has the world by the tail," one coworker stated.

On October 26, 1995, thirteen months since the disappearance of Khristine Smith, Judge Donald Halstead presided over the family court that would determine where Lisa Smith would be temporarily placed. Testimony began at 11:15 A.M. and lasted until just past 6:00 P.M.

After all the testimony had been heard, and the judge had weighed each person's statements. He followed the recommendation of the court-appointed special advocate (CASA) worker and Lisa's attorney. The decision was announced that, for the time being, Lisa Smith would reside with her maternal grandmother, Kay Klein, in Florida. The Smiths' hearts sank. They had hoped that Lisa would be with them, but they were forced to accept the court's decision.

Lisa requested that she be allowed to remain in her foster home through Halloween; therefore, the judge set the transfer date for Friday, November 3, 1995.

Four days before her scheduled departure, Lisa met with her father and her court-approved chaperon at the local McDonald's. The basic topic of conversation was Khristine. Smith stressed to his daughter that he had nothing to do with her mother's disappearance. He repeated his plea of innocence when he spoke with Lisa by phone later that week.

Smith called Lisa to let her know he had an out-of-town business meeting that week, along with other things he had to do, and probably would not see her before she left for Florida.

"Hope you have a nice visit with Grandma Klein," Smith had said, ending the conversation.

Teresa, who had been listening on the extension, was perplexed by Smith's words. Earlier, he had requested a weekend with Lisa in Ohio; then, suddenly, he was too busy to see his little girl. Knowing that in less than a month Smith could be sent to prison for embezzlement, Teresa was shocked to hear he was forgoing one last visit with her before she left for Florida. After all, it was not just for a "visit" but a temporary home until the court decided full guardianship.

With her head down and shoulders stooped, Lisa Smith walked to the gate of the Northwest Airline plane that would be taking her to her grandmother's. She had said most of her good-byes, including telling her classmates she was moving to Florida because "my dad killed my mom."

She gave Teresa one last hug as tears burned her eyes. As the little girl walked down the Jetway accompanied by a flight attendant, Teresa said a little prayer for the young girl who had experienced too much tragedy in her eight short years. She hoped Lisa's life would be filled eventually with happiness and stability. But within three days of Lisa's having arrived in Florida, Kay Klein had called Detective Dylhoff. She related a phone conversation she had had with Russ a couple of days before.

Russ Smith had contacted Kay regarding Lisa visiting him and his parents later in the month for the Thanksgiving holiday. Kay explained to Smith that she didn't believe the visit would be in Lisa's best interest, but he'd been persistent.

"Lisa has just gotten to Florida, and is just getting settled in. I feel that it would be best to start working on Christmas visitation rather than Thanksgiving," Kay had told Smith.

"Russ got very upset and said, 'You better let her come to Ohio so I can see her, or I'll have you back in court!' He stated he didn't know what was going to happen at his November twenty-eighth court date and that he might get locked up for six months. He said Thanksgiving weekend could be the last time he would be able to see Lisa for a while," Kay told Dylhoff.

During their conversation Smith had reminded Kay he had allowed her to see Lisa the prior Thanksgiving, with Kay retorting that he had never allowed her to be alone with her granddaughter. The friction between Kay and Russ was apparent, intensified by early-morning hang-up phone calls Kay was certain were coming from Smith, since his embezzlement hearing had been postponed and Lisa had remained with her for Thanksgiving.

From December 29, 1995, through January 9, 1996, either Russ Smith or his parents called every day to talk with Lisa. One day Kay listened to Lisa's responses to her father as they talked on the phone.

It appeared that Smith had planned to go to Florida for Lisa's birthday. Kay could tell from the expression on her Lisa's face and the tone of her voice that Lisa was very upset. Then Smith evidently changed the conversation to his desire for Lisa to live with him.

"I don't feel safe," Lisa had told her father. "And Mommy didn't just leave me."

Anger boiled within Smith. The one person he

loved more than anyone else was apparently turning away from him because of the one person he hated most. "Your mother left you!" Smith lashed out.

"No! She didn't! She wouldn't just leave like that," Lisa shot back.

"Your mother just left you!" Smith shouted, his words slicing through Lisa's already fragile psyche.

Tears had streamed down Lisa's cheeks as she gulped for air.

Kay Klein had taken the phone from her granddaughter. "This conversation is over," Kay told Russ, and then she hung up the phone.

Another family court hearing regarding Lisa Smith's custody was held, January 9, 1996. Russ Smith had impressed upon the court that he wanted to raise his daughter. He had purchased a house with Julie Moore, holding the deed as joint tenants with full rights of survivorship. They planned to marry and raise her son and his daughter together.

At the conclusion of the hearing, Judge Halstead indicated that it appeared the only barrier keeping Russell Smith from having his daughter returned to him was his alleged involvement in the disappearance of his wife, Khristine Smith. Russ Smith's still-pending charge of embezzlement didn't deter the court from its opinion.

Dylhoff sat silently in the gallery of the courtroom. He feared for Lisa Smith if she was returned to her father. Then the judge put her fate in his hands.

"Detective Dylhoff," Judge Halstead began. "I order you to be at the guardianship hearing set for April twenty-third and twenty-fourth. At that time you should bring all documents in your investigation of the father, Russell Smith."

Even before the final guardianship hearing was held, Lisa Smith was moved from Florida to Ohio. Kay Klein hadn't been able to care for the needs of her granddaughter any easier than she had been able to handle her own daughter. The demands of a young child, the interruption the task had made in her life, was too much for Kay. She shipped Lisa off to the Smiths in Ohio, where the child lived for two months before Detective Dylhoff became aware of the situation.

In early April 1996, Teresa notified Dylhoff that Lisa was in town for a week to visit her father. Russ Smith had called his daughter's former foster mother in hopes she would be able to baby-sit with Lisa while both he and Julie worked. The detective later learned that Smith had contacted other friends and former neighbors to have them pitch in to care for Lisa during her short visit.

Dylhoff was appalled. He called the prosecutor's office and inquired about the last court orders pertaining to visitation between Smith and his daughter. They advised that the visits required supervision; however, there was some discretion left up to the caseworker.

Dylhoff's next call was to the Department of Social Services. He learned that the caseworker assigned the Smith case had approved the unsupervised visits, allowing Lisa to stay with Russ and Julie from Wednesday, April 3, 1996, through Sunday, April 7, 1996. Although Dylhoff expressed his disapproval of any contact between Smith and Lisa without the presence of a chaperon, the caseworker didn't see a problem with the visits.

Dylhoff told the caseworker that he thought it was kind of strange that Smith would have Lisa for an entire week, but one day she spent at school, another day with a foster mother, and then Saturday evening he contacted people he hadn't seen in over a year and wanted them to watch Lisa. Again the caseworker saw no problems with what Smith was doing.

Within six months of Lisa moving to Ohio to live with her grandparents, and two years after the disappearance of Khris Smith, Russ Smith broke his engagement to Julie Moore, leaving Julie wondering why. He quickly became involved with a woman by the name of Mari Norris, the mother of one young daughter. Like most of the women Smith had made contact with since his wife's disappearance, Mari had met him through a personal ad he had placed in the local newspaper.

When Mari spoke with Detective Dylhoff, he could tell she was obviously infatuated with Smith.

Norris explained to Dylhoff the sequence of events Smith had recounted for her concerning his argument with Khris, the pulling of the plug wires on her car, the damage she had done to the bathroom, and his departure from the house to give Khris time to cool off. She declared to Dylhoff that she believed Smith had done nothing wrong, although her suspicions had been raised when he told her that the only evidence or proof the police had was the damaged bathroom.

"He feels that he is being followed all of the time and that his phone is tapped," Mari told Dylhoff.

Dylhoff recognized the now-familiar signs of Smith's keen paranoia.

"He feels that he is going to be arrested very soon. He wants to be charged so he can have a jury trial and have this all over with. It appears to be wearing him down. He said that he'll probably have to sell his car and his house, but that he wanted a jury trial," Mari stated.

"He also thinks Khristine was putting money away on the side because she basically controlled the finances at the house. He feels that she probably left with somewhere around twenty thousand dollars," Mari added.

Dylhoff was aware that Khris had kept the family financial records. When he had checked the Smiths' bank records for the eight-month period, just prior to her disappearance, Khris had written 303 checks, with Russ Smith having written only six. The Smiths' credit cards had also been paid off each month. But since Khris's absence, Russ Smith's credit cards held large balances.

As the conversation with Dylhoff was ending, Mari Norris admitted her sisters were concerned about her relationship with Smith. She herself was concerned about things she had been hearing, but her concerns apparently failed to override her sense that Smith was honest, sincere, and fun to be with.

One week after initially talking with Mari, Dylhoff received a frantic phone call from her. She demanded to know why Dylhoff had called the Department of Social Services on her.

"Where did you get that idea?" Dylhoff asked, puzzled by the implication.

"They contacted me and wouldn't reveal their source," Mari said quickly.

"I didn't contact them and have no knowledge of them being contacted," Dylhoff stated.

Norris told Dylhoff she had broken off her relationship with Russell Smith and had no information that could help him out with the investigation.

"I just want out of what's going on," Mari said anxiously.

Dylhoff again assured Mari that he had nothing to do with DSS being called, but that if someone had contacted them, it was probably because of concern about her young daughter being around Smith. As she had before, the emotionally charged woman assured the detective she had never left her daughter alone with Smith. Before hanging up, she reiterated that her relationship with Smith was off and that she wanted nothing to do with him or anything surrounding him. The call ended as abruptly as it had started.

Russ Smith had attended his final court hearing on embezzlement charges. He had garnered a probated sentence, rather than the jail time he had expected. Smith felt confident that he could begin to move forward, to make plans for the future.

With Julie Moore out of his life, and Mari Norris fed up with the negative disruption he had brought to their relationship, Russ Smith again turned to the personal ads. This time the ad read "Big Flirt" in bold print. The body of the notice was much like that written under "Quixotic." But when Dylhoff called the recorded Dateline message, he heard Russ Smith's voice. Smith called himself Lee, described his physical characteristics, and listed a few of his personality traits that included being quiet at times and outrageously outgoing and adventurous at other times. Smith listed his hobbies as boating, golf, and the proverbial pastime listed in almost every single male's ad, "walks on the beach." He claimed if he had one wish it would be to make people smile. Smith told callers he was interested in their physical appearance, things they enjoying doing, and their occupation. He categorized himself as a playboy, even admitting that if he were on a date that wasn't going well he would venture out to meet somebody else that might have caught his eye.

Dylhoff shook his head slightly as he hung up the phone. It was hard to believe any woman would respond to a man as arrogant as Russ Smith.

Nearly four years after Khristine Smith was last seen in Portage, Michigan, life for Russ Smith had changed dramatically. His daughter had been legally adopted by his parents; he was on probation for embezzlement and was being investigated for tax fraud; he had moved to Florida and was engaged to yet another woman who believed his lies and half-truths.

The one constant that remained in the Khristine Smith investigation was Detective Randy Dylhoff. He continued to persist in checking the infrequent leads that came across his desk or in reinterviewing a witness he thought may have remembered something earlier forgotten. Perhaps it was simply his dedication to the job, or his desire to find a child's mother; maybe it was because he knew he had once had Russ Smith in his grasp, so close to a full confession, and one lousy mistake had allowed him to slip away.

On August 28, 1998, exactly one month shy of four years since Khris's disappearance, Dylhoff and Detective Romanak traveled to Cridersville, Ohio, to visit with Lisa Smith.

When the detectives arrived just after dark, Lisa was still away at cheerleading practice. Both Roger and Linda Smith, Lisa's grandparents, told the detectives that Lisa was doing well. Linda said Khris was seldom mentioned in their home, but every once in a while Lisa would say, "My mom used to do that" or "My mom did it that way," whenever her grandmother would remind her of the mother who had been gone for so long.

Lisa had lost so much. Her mother was gone; her father was building a new life with another woman and her child; grandmother Klein no longer wrote or called to see how she was doing. Lisa's psychologist told the Smiths it was as if Lisa had a big bubble around her with everything that had happened in her life. The psychologist warned that the bubble could burst at any time.

Lisa walked in shortly after the detectives arrived at her grandparents' home. Dylhoff was pleased to see her. She had grown considerably and was now eleven years old. When Dylhoff explained that they were still investigating the disappearance of her mother, her physical expressions gave away her emotional despair. Her eyes watered. Her posture shrank. Her voice softened, but she didn't cry. Perhaps her tears had all been spilled. Possibly, she had given up hope of ever finding her mother or the truth about her father's involvement.

Part 2

Chapter 21

In the four years since Khris Smith vanished, the *Discovery* shuttle docked with the Mir station for the first time, the Oklahoma City Federal Building was bombed, O.J. Simpson was found not guilty, Bill Clinton won a second term, and Princess Diana died.

The Smith case had come to an absolute standstill. No one had heard from Khris Smith for more than four years. Russ Smith had slyly averted giving a full confession, and what Smith had confided to Dylhoff couldn't be used against him in a court of law because Smith hadn't been read his Miranda rights. Smith had moved to Navarre, Florida, to begin a new life far away from the persistent glare of authorities and the media. He appeared to believe he was untouchable and had gotten away with murder. But Smith's false sense of assuredness was to be short-lived.

In 1998, funded by a federal grant, a cold-case homicide squad was formed in Kalamazoo County. The multijurisdictional task force was comprised of men from the Kalamazoo County Sheriff's Department, the Kalamazoo Police Department, and the Portage Police Department. Administrative assistance was provided by Kalamazoo Township.

Team members included Richard Mattison, Mike Brown, Dan Weston, Mike Werkema, Ron Petroski, and Greg Hatter. This group of six highly skilled and dedicated officers was assigned the task of combining efforts to investigate complex cases that had baffled police departments within the entire county. They would become known as the Cold Case Career Criminal Apprehension Team (CCCCAT).

Sergeant Mike Werkema was one of those assigned to CCCCAT by the Kalamazoo PD. Werkema, a veteran homicide officer, had followed the Khris Smith case from the beginning. He had even contacted Detective Dylhoff at one point during the investigation, offering information he had concerning Smith. Like Dylhoff, Werkema was convinced Russ Smith was responsible for not only the disappearance, but also the death of his wife.

Sitting at the table in what would become known as the "the nest," an undisclosed office set up for use by the newly formed investigative force, Werkema detailed the events leading up to the disappearance of Khris Smith. He described Russ Smith as a devoted family man prior to his wife's mysterious desertion and his uncharacteristic conduct following her disappearance.

"He began frequenting strip joints, he put ads in the personals, he relinquished parental rights to his daughter following allegations of child molestation, and he was convicted on four counts of felony embezzlement," Werkema reported.

Werkema leaned his muscular arms on the table as he told the men about statements made by Lisa Smith to detectives concerning her parents' arguments and the damaged condition of her mother's bathroom.

As Werkema presented each piece of information pertaining to the Smith incident, excitement and anticipation danced in his eyes. His straight brown hair moved slightly as he turned his head to face various team members during his discourse. The corners of his mouth turned upward as he began encouraging his new cohorts to take on the Khris Smith disappearance as CCCCAT's maiden case. Werkema displayed his usual robust enthusiasm whenever he sensed that a new case could come to full fruition.

"Investigation is just talking to people. We'll go out and reinterview everyone connected with the case," Werkema told them.

Werkema knew that the span of years could easily dull the memories of those who had initially been questioned, but he also knew that situations change. Perhaps someone, who at the outset had been reluctant to talk or who had defended Smith without full knowledge of the facts, would now be able to give them information essential to solving the case. The sly detective also planned to play the tape recording Detective Dylhoff had made of his conversation with Smith. The tape was not admissible in a court of law, but there was nothing barring the CCCCAT from playing it for others to hear. Werkema decided every person they talked to during the investigation would know Russ Smith was an admitted killer. Werkema was even prepared to play the tape for Smith's parents in an effort to draw them into helping with the investigation. Hopefully, hearing their son confess to murder would convince them the boy they had called Rusty as a child had been lying to them for four years.

Once the cold-case squad unanimously agreed to tackle the Smith case, the six investigators began to strategize. Captain Daniel Weston, of the Kalamazoo

Department of Public Safety and head of the CCC-CAT, assigned specific duties to each of his team members. In October 1998, four years and one week after Khris Smith vanished from her Portage, Michigan, home, the first of many unsolved crimes was tackled by the CCCCAT.

Mike Werkema went back to the very beginning of the case, executing his plan of talking to everyone ever connected with Khris Smith. His first interview was with Tom Huss, the Smith's neighbor and local fireman who first reported Khris Smith as a missing person.

Huss told Werkema that after the disappearance of Khris Smith and the report he made to the Portage Police Department, he had conducted a fire inspection in a local bait-and-tackle shop owned by Phillip Miller. In his conversation with Miller, Huss had mentioned the incident that occurred over the previous weekend with his neighbors, Khris and Russ Smith. Miller offhandedly remarked that a person had been in the shop the previous week inquiring about the depth of water in areas of Sugarloaf Lake. Miller wondered if it could have possibly been the same person Huss spoke of.

The following day, on September 22, 1998, Mike Werkema visited Phillip Miller at his business. The detective asked Miller if he recalled the conversation with Huss. Miller said he did remember and, in fact, had later seen a story in the paper about the Smith woman's disappearance. He'd recognized a photo of Russ Smith as the man who had inquired about the waters in Sugarloaf Lake.

Phillip Miller was a retired police officer with over twenty years' service. It was his habit to know people's

faces and names. He definitely remembered Russ
Smith. Smith, like so many of Miller's patrons, had
asked where the fish were biting in Sugarloaf Lake.
When Miller gave Smith a location, he asked how
deep the waters were in that specific area.

"Do you know any other deeper spots in Sugarloaf
Lake?" Smith had asked.

"You'll have to go into Little Sugarloaf Lake, where
the lake's much deeper. There are some spots there
that are forty to fifty feet deep. There's a channel that
connects Sugarloaf to Little Sugarloaf Lake," Miller
had informed Smith.

Miller told Werkema he thought the whole conversation with Smith had been very "off." He recalled
watching the man who had bought some wax worms
drive away in a pickup, pulling no boat.

"I wondered, why is he asking me where the deep
spots on the lake are and how is he going to fish these
deep spots if he doesn't have a boat?" Miller said.

Miller recalled that his conversation with Smith
took place in late September because it was the first
week in October when Tom Huss was in the store.

"Why didn't you think to contact the police?"
Werkema inquired.

"I talked to Tom Huss about the conversation with
Smith. I believed Huss was going to advise the police. I
assumed you already knew, and didn't think anymore
about it," Miller said.

"Are you *certain* the man who you had that conversation with was Russ Smith?" Werkema asked.

Miller assured the detective it was, indeed, Russ
Smith.

Werkema was pleased with the Miller interview.
Instinctually he knew there was a lot more people

out there just like Phillip Miller, people who had
information about Russ Smith but who had never
been questioned. Werkema's natural zeal for justice
intensified.

Detective Sergeant Rich Mattison, a tall, brawny,
experienced officer, had drawn the assignment of
speaking to Kurt Piska, a coworker of Russ Smith's
at Sears at the time Khris was reported missing. Mattison's questions concentrated on a .380 automatic
handgun Piska had purchased at an Indiana gun
show for Smith.

Piska recalled attending the gun show at the Fort
Wayne Coliseum, along with Smith and Homer Hardesty, another of Smith's coworkers, on March 10,
1991, 3½ years before Khris Smith vanished. Piska,
who had just moved to Indiana, didn't have an Indiana driver's license so he couldn't purchase a weapon.
Smith didn't have a permit to purchase. Homer Hardesty, using his concealed weapons permit license,
purchased two handguns; one for Piska and one for
Smith.

Davis Industries of Chino, California, had manu-
factured both guns. They were identical model
P-380s, chrome-plated, with black plastic grips. They
each held five shots.

Detective Mattison's next call was to Homer Hardesty. He confirmed the transactions among himself,
the gun dealer, Smith, and Piska. Hardesty had purchased the two guns, given them to Smith and Piska,
and received seventy-five dollars from each of them.
He recalled the handguns as being cheaply made.
Others would describe them as a lightweight lady's
gun or, more derogatorily, as a piece of junk.

Mattison made notes in the Smith file being main-

tained by the CCCCAT. The detective knew from
reading the field notes from the original investigation
that Smith owned a number of guns. He may have
even fancied himself as a gun collector.

Chapter 22

Sergeants Mike Werkema and Mike Brown made the 3½-hour trip to Lima, Ohio, from Kalamazoo, Michigan. They had requested Roger and Linda Smith, along with Lisa, meet them there. The Smiths' home in Cridersville was within easy driving distance and the detectives wanted a neutral place for their initial encounter. Werkema knew the Smiths had been harassed by reporters and taunted by curious townspeople. There was no need to create an opportunity for further speculation. Now that the task force had Julie Moore's statements, along with the tape of Russ Smith's confession to Randy Dylhoff, they were anxious to talk with the Smiths.

Werkema, just under six feet one and solidly built, along with Brown, who was about six feet, with a muscular physique, were far less intimidating to Lisa Smith than the six-five towering figure of Randy Dylhoff. Brown and Werkema were dressed casually; Brown was in a suit, Werkema in short-sleeved shirt and slacks. They didn't want to look intimidating. They didn't look like cops.

Werkema's style was to make his subjects feel comfortable. "I use the warm and fuzzy approach," he'd said.

Werkema flashed his engaging smile to set Lisa, now

eleven years old, at ease. She looked younger than her eleven years. She wore a white T-shirt, overalls, and her dirty blond hair pulled back in a ponytail. Her youth was a strong contrast to her white-haired grandparents, who, after raising their own children, were now rearing Lisa.

It was obvious to the investigators that Lisa was well cared for by the Smiths. She appeared bright and alert, and although she was not anxious to talk about her mother's disappearance and her father's possible involvement, she was willing to listen.

Werkema pulled a small tape recorder from his breast pocket and set it on the table between himself and Lisa.

"There's a tape we want to play for you. A lady who talked to you four years ago," Werkema explained.

Debbie Orosz's voice soon filled the room.

"Hi, Lisa. You're probably wondering why I'm talking to you. It's been almost four years since we've seen each other. The reason I'm speaking to you, Lisa, is to introduce you to a new team of officers who are trying their very best to find out about your mom. I want you to be able to trust them, not to be afraid of them, just to be trusting of them. I know this must be really hard for you to talk about. At the age you were when this happened, it must have been really hard to talk about it. Now that you're eleven, and all grown-up, you must see things differently.

"Your mommy really loved you, Lisa. She talked on many occasions of how proud she was of you. I know this will bring back memories that are probably painful to you, but I want you to trust these new officers. Tell them anything and everything you can to help them. Help them in the search for your mom. It's always important to tell the truth.

"Honey, I want you to know, we'll be here in Kalamazoo. We'll do anything and everything we can in your search for your mom. Before I say good-bye, I want you to know if there is ever any time you want to talk to someone, remember, I'm only a phone call away. I love you and I miss you. Bye for now."

From the confused expression on Lisa Smith's face, Werkema could tell she didn't recall the woman who spoke to her on the tape.

"It's been a long time," Werkema said with a nervous chuckle. "As I said, my name is Mike," Werkema continued.

"Two Mikes," Roger Smith interrupted. Uneasy laughter came from everyone in the room but Lisa.

"We're a new team of investigators, each working forty hours a week on this case," Werkema said.

"Can I ask you a question?" Linda Smith broke in. "Are you from Kalamazoo?"

Werkema explained that all of the cold-case squad members were from Kalamazoo County. They were working together to bring resolution to unsolved cases.

Roger Smith expressed his belief that the Michigan State Police had been involved with his son's case at one time, and he wondered why suddenly this new local team was investigating Russ.

Brown explained that the case of Khris's disappearance had been turned over to them and that the state police had investigated Russ for sales tax fraud. They'd had nothing to do with the case involving the Smiths' daughter-in-law, with the exception of offering support during the original investigation.

Werkema took a folded piece of paper from one of

the two file folders on the table in front of him and handed it to Lisa, who sat between her grandmother and grandfather. "That's a letter from Heather. Do you remember Heather? She sent you a letter. You can read it later," Werkema said as he handed it to Lisa.

Lisa's expression again reflected the lack of recognition as it had when listening to Debbie Orosz on tape. Heather Orosz, like her mother, had become no more than a faded memory.

"This isn't easy, obviously," Werkema stated in his soft-spoken voice. "Our goal is to find your mother. We want closure to it for everybody, especially for you. We know today is the anniversary date and we know that's a very special day in your life. We also know this—[there's] a particular time in the past that you've chosen to talk to people about what happened, or what you think happened. Rather than waiting and coming a week from now, we thought this was a better time. We assumed, because of the past, that you'd be thinking of your mother, what happened, and that this would be the day to talk to you. We chose this day."

"I know you did," Roger Smith said critically.

Werkema and Brown backed off from continuing their direct approach and began talking to Lisa and the Smiths about her school, her cheerleading, and her new friends in Ohio. Werkema even talked about his seventh-grade son, who played junior-high football in Kalamazoo. He was making it personal, setting Lisa and, hopefully, the Smiths at ease.

Looking at Lisa, Werkema asked, "Do you think you can talk about it? I want to know what you think. I want you to be honest. Very honest."

Lisa sat slumped in her seat, looking down at the Kleenex she twisted in her hands.

"Everybody on this side of the room is your family," Werkema said, motioning to the Smiths, "and they love you. Regardless of what you think, they'll still love you. Does that make sense?"

Lisa looked at Werkema and nodded without speaking.

"I'm hoping you can clarify some of your past statements and I'm hoping I can even tell you some things. The unfortunate thing is that we're bringing bad news to you because we're investigating a bad memory. Something sad. Something there's no closure to. It's not going to be a happy talk, I know that. I gotta believe you want to know what happened to your mother and you want to know where she is, don't you? Is that important to you? Is that important to your grandma and grandpa?" Werkema asked.

"Mom and Dad," Roger Smith corrected quickly. The Smiths had been Lisa's parents for more than a year and had taken on the more authoritarian titles after her legal adoption.

Werkema told Lisa he had confidence that the people now working on her mother's case were going to be able to find the closure he believed she wanted. He offered her the opportunity to ask him and Sergeant Brown any questions she may have, while they attempted to get answers to their own questions. He assured her they would hold nothing back from her.

Roger Smith became belligerent, saying that if they were some kind of special task force they should have all the information on the case. Brown assured the protective grandfather that indeed they did have all the records at their disposal.

"I only see two little files laying there," Roger Smith

said, referring to the files lying on the table in front of Brown and his partner.

"I assure you, we have all four hundred and fifty-two pages," Brown replied.

"I have absolutely no idea what's in that case file," Roger Smith stated.

"What I have here are past interviews with Lisa," Werkema replied, flipping open the file before him. "I have Khris's letter she left for your son and notes from the initial investigation."

Roger Smith stared at Werkema and Brown. It was obvious to the two detectives that Smith remained firmly behind the innocence of his son.

"We also have some new information we've uncovered during our investigation. That's why we feel it's important to talk to you. Is that okay?" Werkema asked, hoping he had reduced the tension that radiated from Roger Smith.

"If she doesn't want to answer any questions, she doesn't have to," Roger Smith insisted.

"Absolutely," Brown assured him.

Werkema breathed a sigh of relief. The first hurdle in their attempt to get Lisa Smith to talk about the day her mother disappeared had been overcome. He turned his attention to the sandy-blond-haired girl before him.

"Do you hear from your dad often?" Werkema asked.

"Yes," Lisa replied in the soft, high-pitched voice of a young child.

Lisa said she heard from her father almost every day, in the evening right before her bedtime. Roger Smith corrected his granddaughter, stating that Russ didn't call every night.

"What do you remember about that day?" Werkema asked.

"That when I got home from school, she was gone," Lisa said, her voice breaking and tears filling her eyes.

"What did your dad tell you?" Werkema coaxed.

"That she left," Lisa replied, taking in a deep breath while tears softly rolled down her unblemished cheeks.

Mike Brown began recapping the events of September 28, 1994, which had been determined during Dylhoff's investigation. Lisa nodded in agreement as he mentioned arriving home, being told to pack a bag, and instructed not to go in her bathroom as her father talked on the phone. Lisa sniffed frequently as she tried to hold back the tears.

Lisa described disobeying her father and entering the bathroom with a key from over the door frame. She confirmed that the shower doors and showerhead were broken and splinters of wood were scattered about the floor. She claimed she saw nothing in the sink. She had been told by her father that her mother had damaged the bathroom.

In discussing the drive to Ohio that evening, Lisa told the detectives there was very little said between her and her father. She talked about her bike being in the back of the truck, along with her pet rabbit, Buster, but she couldn't seem to recall if there was a barrel in the bed of the pickup or not.

It had become obvious to Werkema that Lisa Smith was afraid. She feared incriminating her father, but most of all she feared losing her grandparents and the right to be raised by them.

"Do you know where your mom is?" Brown asked.

"No," Lisa said softly, sniffling as before.

"Any thoughts of where she might be?" Werkema asked.

"No."

Lisa laid her head on her grandmother's shoulder for comfort. Linda Smith put her arm around Lisa. She patted Lisa's left arm while Roger Smith stroked the other.

"You know, people make mistakes, Lisa," Brown stated. "And sometimes they get scared after they make a mistake and they do things that make it look like they meant to do what they did. It just makes it look worse than it is. You know what I mean? We know everybody makes mistakes."

Brown paused.

"Did you ever tell anyone that family doesn't tell on family?" Brown asked.

Lisa shook her head.

"Do you think about your mom?" Werkema asked, changing the focus in an attempt to get Lisa to open up. The girl rested her elbows on the table and her head in her hands as Linda Smith stroked her back. When she said she often thought of her mother, Werkema asked, "Do you think your mom's alive?"

"Yes."

"Why do you think that?" Werkema prodded.

"I just do," Lisa replied through her sniffles.

"Have there been any calls?" Werkema asked.

"No."

"Do you hope to see her again?"

"Yes."

"If something terrible happened to your mother, would you want us to find out?" Werkema questioned.

Lisa nodded yes as she twisted a Kleenex in her hands.

"Would you want to know if something terrible happened to your mother?" Werkema continued.

Lisa again nodded.

"If something terrible happened to your mother, would you want us to catch the person who did it?" Werkema questioned, leading to his purpose for being there.

Linda Smith removed her eyeglasses and wiped tears from her eyes. The possibility of Khris's tragic fate was difficult for her to handle.

"If we caught that person, what would you want us to do?"

"I don't know," Lisa mumbled.

Werkema returned to the subject of the bathroom sink, asking the eleven-year-old if she remembered stating in a previous interview that she had seen blood in the sink. She claimed she didn't recall making the statement.

Brown inquired if Lisa's parents had been arguing the day her mother left, earlier in the week, or at the family wedding the Saturday before.

"I can tell you one thing, they didn't sit with the rest of the family, they moved away from the family."

The Smiths were growing tired of the questions being asked of their granddaughter. They had seen Lisa questioned and requestioned for years by police, attorneys, and judges. They were trying to make a stable life for her. They didn't want her to be pointed at, or made fun of by others, because Khris had suddenly vanished.

Werkema and Brown understood their feelings. They had empathy for Lisa and what she had been put through, but they knew the child needed to know what happened to her mother. She needed to be relieved of the burdens she carried on her young shoulders.

"We are truth seekers," Werkema told the Smiths. "We are here to find the truth. Do you want this to go on?"

"Sure, we'd like to know where she's at," Roger Smith said, his wife concurring. "I know the people in Michigan think she's dead, but I honestly don't know."

Werkema, the father of four, asked the Smiths a difficult question: "If you knew your son was involved, would you share that information?"

"If I knew that he was involved, I would," Roger Smith said.

"If someone had that information, would you want to know?" Werkema asked.

"If they could prove it to me. But they'd have to prove it," Roger Smith answered.

"What would it take to prove it to you?" Werkema asked.

"I guess I'd have to see a body or he'd have to tell me," Roger Smith stated.

Werkema was inwardly delighted with Smith's response. He knew he couldn't give him a body, but he had his son's own voice on tape admitting to the murder of his wife.

"What if there wasn't a body, but Russ told you he did it?" Brown interjected.

"Told me? I guess I'd have to believe him," Roger Smith replied.

"Let's say he told you he did it. Would you want him to go through the system?" Werkema asked.

"I'd want to know all of the facts," Smith's father hedged. "I'd want to know: Did you do it on purpose?

Did you fight? Did you hit her and she fell and hit her head? I would like to know all the facts."

"That's why we're here, to seek the truth," Werkema said.

"We've been kept in the dark," Roger Smith said.

"The only information we've gotten was in the Kalamazoo papers," Linda Smith added.

Werkema explained that they were treating the investigation as a homicide. Their goal was to find Khris and let her have a proper burial. And they wanted to find out what happened on that day in early fall 1994. He told the Smiths the team wanted to bring resolution, as painful as that might be for them.

The detective continued by explaining that there were consequences to all actions. The parents may wonder "what did I do wrong," but that wasn't a factor in this instance. Werkema admitted Russ was their only suspect, suggesting that perhaps he'd snapped; they didn't know for sure. That was their purpose, to find the truth about what happened to Khris. He reaffirmed their goal of talking to anyone and everyone who could give them information that would lead to the conclusion of the case.

"You wanted factual information?" Werkema asked. "I can give you factual information today before we leave this room. So you have no doubt in your mind who's involved with Khristine's death."

Werkema and Brown watched the faces of the three Smiths as they digested the statement. The contrast of their reactions was astounding.

Lisa's face radiated relief. It was as if a weight had been lifted from her narrow shoulders. Her expression seemed to say, "Someone else knows my secret."

In sharp disparity the Smiths' faces reflected doubt

and disbelief at what Werkema told them. They weren't ready to accept that their son was a killer.

"There will be no question in your mind. Absolutely no question," Werkema assured.

"That I don't understand," Roger Smith said, appearing confused. "If you have proof positive . . ."

"Because of a technicality, because proper procedures weren't followed, there's a high possibility that the evidence we have won't be allowed into court," Werkema attempted to explain. "To put it bluntly, an error on the investigator's part."

"If you have that kind of information, I think you should use it," Roger Smith said with skepticism.

"Oh, we will. I'm prepared to let you hear that information," Werkema said. He felt certain that when the Smiths heard their son's verbal confession, they would help them persuade Russ to provide information on the whereabouts of Khristine's body.

"I'm not sure I want to hear it," Russ Smith's father said honestly.

"That's why I asked you earlier, what would it take?" Werkema quickly responded.

"From him," Roger Smith said, his voice reflecting the pain he was feeling. "I'd have to hear it from him."

"From him," Werkema said.

"If he's told you, why hasn't he told me?" Roger Smith asked, obviously hurt by his son's lack of candor.

"He did not tell us," Brown interjected.

"He told Randy," Werkema stated, speaking of Detective Dylhoff of the Portage PD.

"I can't believe that if I told someone, like Mr. Brown, something like that, that my ass wouldn't be sitting in a cell right now," Roger Smith said.

"The law states that if a person is in custody, every

time you talk to that person, you have to reread him his Miranda rights. That it's your right to have an attorney, et cetera. So every time you go back and talk to that person, you have to read him his constitutional rights. That's the law," Werkema explained. "We want your help; we need your help," Werkema pleaded. "Make no mistake; when we leave here you'll know in your mind and your heart who the person who killed Khris is."

"So you're saying Randy has it on tape?" Roger Smith asked.

"Yep," Werkema responded.

"He didn't have an attorney present?" Smith asked.

"Nope."

"Why?" Roger Smith wanted to know.

"Because, at the time, Randy was playing messenger between your son and the prosecutor. Trying to work out a deal. Randy was trying to be 'Mr. Nice Guy' to your son, to get the best deal for him. He was running back and forth, trying to make a great deal, so Russ would tell us all the facts. When it got down to it, the prosecutor said, 'Until we know what happened, we can't give a deal.' Dylhoff was working to get a low charge," Werkema detailed.

Roger Smith began talking about domestic violence he'd seen on TV and how mistakes are made, how people work to cover something up and end up making matters worse.

"We know who the killer is," Werkema stressed. "That half of the case is resolved. The half we're working on is, where is Khris? When we take care of that part, then we can get the judicial part done."

Werkema glanced toward Lisa. Her tears had dried. She appeared calm, almost relieved at Werkema's statement. Linda Smith's face, on the other hand, showed the worry lines of a distressed mother.

"I have mixed emotions," Roger Smith said, bewilderment clearly on his face. He didn't want to believe what Werkema and Brown were telling him. He didn't want to believe his son was a killer. Roger and Linda Smith were clearly in denial.

"I know what can happen," Roger Smith said. "I watch *Unsolved Mysteries.* Sometimes people are gone for years; then they show up."

"Khris isn't going to show up," Brown stated flatly.

"If you've got that tape, I don't want to see it," Roger Smith said emphatically.

Werkema understood Smith's reluctance; after all, as a father he would naturally be hesitant to hear bad news from one of his sons. Werkema assured Smith he understood. Then he guaranteed that the new task force was going ahead full throttle to bring the case to a successful conclusion.

"If what you are saying is true, I think it must have been an accident," Roger Smith said.

"I think there was an argument and Russ must have snapped," Werkema said. "We don't think it was planned. Just a spur-of-the-moment thing."

For the first time during the conversation, Linda Smith vigorously spoke out.

"And I don't believe that molestation thing. She loves her father. Just because she wanted her hair blond and her father tried to color it, turning it orange, does that mean he's a bad father? At age three she was platinum blond. She just wanted to be blond again," Linda Smith stated, minimizing her son's prior actions.

"We're only here to talk about the situation with

Khris; we have nothing to do with any other cases against Russ," Werkema assured Mrs. Smith.

Werkema asked the Smiths not to share with Russ their conversation, reminding them that in the past Russ had made reference to hurting himself. The last thing Werkema wanted was for Russ Smith to take his own life without revealing where Khris's body could be found.

"I've laid all our cards on the table," Werkema said. "It's extremely important that Russ not know what was said in our conversation. Do I have your word?"

Werkema scrutinized Roger Smith closely. He wondered if he could be trusted to keep their discussion secret.

Roger Smith agreed not to share the context of their talk with his son. Werkema and Brown could only hope he kept his word.

As the interview was winding down, Werkema asked Lisa to keep a journal of any thoughts or questions she may have regarding her mother. If she remembered anything she hadn't already told them, he asked that she jot it down in her journal.

The eleven-year-old had become comfortable with Werkema. She smiled, even gave a little laugh, as she told him she already had three diaries and would be happy to keep one for him. Even the Smiths' demeanor had changed—they too agreed to be as helpful as possible.

As the Smiths left the small interview room that had become unbearably warm for Mrs. Smith, Sergeant Brown held back to talk with Lisa.

Brown and Lisa were alone in the unadorned interview room, which held only three chairs, a small square table, and a calendar, which hung on the wall.

Speaking in a soft tone, Brown told Lisa that family was important. Her mother was important.

"It's important that we find [your] mom so we can bury her," Brown said, "so you can go and pay your respects to your mom. I think she deserves that, don't you?"

"Yes," Lisa replied.

"You have to understand that if your dad told you to keep a secret, that you couldn't tell anybody, he wasn't thinking right. I don't want you to be scared of your dad. He made a mistake. You know that. We have to find your mom and bring her home to bury her. You know your mom's dead, don't you?"

Lisa's earlier congenial mood with Mike Werkema had turned solemn. She mumbled a response to Brown's question that was inaudible.

"We need you to help us, Lisa. We need you to tell us anything you know," Brown encouraged. "I'm sure it was a mistake. They probably got into an argument and things got out of hand. We know your daddy tried to make a deal with Randy and we know he admitted he hurt your mommy," Brown said. "Your daddy isn't a bad person. He made a mistake. I'm sure he loved your mom. But sometimes people do stupid things."

Lisa began to sniffle as she had during the beginning of the interview with Werkema.

"You know your mother didn't do that damage to the bathroom, don't you? She loved that house," Brown continued.

"We had that house especially built for us," Lisa said with pride.

"Will you promise me something?" Brown asked. "And I'll promise you something."

"Yes," Lisa replied.

"If you think of something, will you call and tell me? You have my card. If I have to, I'll drive down and we'll talk. Okay?" Brown asked.

"Yes," Lisa replied.

"And I'll let you know what happens. I'll make sure that you and Mom and Dad (the Smiths) are the first ones to know anything. Is that all right?"

"Yes."

Lisa seemed willing to work with Brown and Werkema, but only time would tell if she could overcome the fear of losing her father and tell them what she knew about her mother's death.

Chapter 23

Julie Moore, former girlfriend and live-in partner of Russ Smith, was high on the list of people to be contacted. Sergeant Mike Werkema hoped that Julie, who had believed in Smith's innocence and defended his character early in the investigation, would now be more willing to talk about the man who jilted her and moved to Florida. He hoped the fact that Smith was now engaged to another woman and living with her and her young daughter would have an effect on Julie. After all, he figured, "there's no wrath like a woman scorned."

The initial contact with Julie Moore was made in late 1998. She was still in denial concerning Smith's guilt. But once Julie listened to the tape of Smith talking with Dylhoff, conversations she had had with Smith during their months together came crashing back. It all became clear. The man she'd once loved was a killer.

Detectives requested she write a statement pertaining to her relationship with Smith and what she knew about the disappearance of his wife. Julie Moore penned an eye-opening eighteen-page letter for the cold-case homicide detectives.

Julie explained that a couple of months into the relationship Smith told her a story about Khris and what happened the day of her disappearance. Julie had been pressuring Smith, asking questions about his wife. She stated she believed Smith had only told her what she wanted to hear, just enough to pacify her. The minute Smith had finished his story, Julie claimed to have thought it was an elaborately made-up tale.

According to Julie's letter, from the beginning of her relationship with Smith, she had thought he had something to do with Khris's disappearance. When she would bring up the possibility, he would merely laugh, telling her she was being silly. Julie, falling in love with Smith, had assured him she wasn't there to judge him but to support him and be his friend.

The tone of Julie's letter turned from accusing to angry when she spoke of Detective Randy Dylhoff and the conversations she had with him concerning Smith. Moore stated that Dylhoff assured her (underlining the word "assured" for emphasis) that she was in no danger and that he actually liked Russ Smith. He thought Smith was a good man who "just lost it with Khris, their fight ending in Russ killing Khris." Moore claimed Dylhoff told her he thought Khris's death had been an accident and that Russ had panicked, trying to lie his way out of it. She also claimed Dylhoff insisted he wasn't there in an attempt to break them up, assuring her that Smith would need her more than ever when the situation came to a close.

Julie Moore's letter made accusations about Dylhoff lying to her and her intense distrust of the Portage cop. She claimed that everything she heard about Russ Smith came directly from Dylhoff. He had even mentioned how the police had messed up the investigation, but had given no details.

Julie's letter took on a lighter quality when she wrote about the daily entries she had chronicled in her diary: things like bike riding, Rollerblading, swimming, fishing, dinners, movies, and vacationing, which she, her young son, and Smith had all enjoyed together. She claimed *everything* she wrote in her diary was positive, assuring the readers of her letter that there was absolutely no negative entry in the journal. Julie wanted them to know Smith had never expressed anger or lost his temper with her. He had always understood and supported her.

Werkema worried. He thought listening to the tape of Smith's confession had done the trick in convincing Julie to tell everything she knew about Smith and his wife's disappearance. Werkema was beginning to have his doubts.

As the sergeant read on, it became evident that Smith's pleasant treatment of Julie and her son wasn't just for her enjoyment. Sometime into the relationship—Julie supposed when Russ thought he could trust her—Smith had asked her to call Randy Dylhoff and tell him she had seen Khris. She had refused, on more than one occasion.

Evidently, Julie also didn't believe the accusations made against Smith in relationship to his daughter. Julie claimed there was absolutely no signs of sexual abuse going on with Lisa after she came into the picture. However, she did admit that by the time she entered Smith's life, Lisa was already living with a foster family, and Khris had been gone for six months.

Moore described a home video Smith had once shown her of a happy-faced little girl jumping on the bed. Julie claimed she told Smith she hoped and prayed he hadn't done anything (sexual) to his little girl. Smith, in turn, assured Julie he hadn't and even the thought of it made him sick to his stomach. Julie insisted Russ Smith had never gotten close to her son in "that way."

According to Julie Moore, Smith had volunteered to let her read all of the police reports and newspaper articles he had saved concerning the accusations against him. Julie had even told Dylhoff that God had put her into Russ Smith's life and he was very good to her. But Dylhoff had disagreed, repeatedly telling her Smith was incapable of loving his daughter, his family, or her. He was just using them for his own purposes. Julie was unaware that Dylhoff was describing the characteristics of a man with narcissistic personality disorder.

Five-and-a-half pages into the letter written by Julie Moore to the cold-case squad, she finally began to relate the story Smith had told her concerning the events that led to his second wife's disappearance.

Moore began by stating that Smith told her he knew Khris was cheating on him, and that she wanted to leave and planned to take Lisa with her. Smith had told Julie he would do *anything* to prevent that from happening. He'd do whatever it took.

Julie's letter detailed Russ Smith's description of his argument with Khris. He claimed Khris went into the bedroom, got a gun, and came back to where he was waiting. According to Julie, Smith claimed Khris was going to shoot him. They struggled, with Russ Smith gaining control of the gun. Instead of walking away, Russ Smith had turned the gun on his wife and fired.

Smith knew he had to get things cleaned up before Lisa got home. He told Julie he talked with someone in Ohio who would help him cover up what he had done. Smith asserted that while he was a police officer in Ohio, he had saved a little girl's life and it was that little girl's father whom he had contacted to help him. Smith alleged that the man worked at a funeral home, in cremation, and he paid this man to "look the other way" while Russ did the actual burning of his wife's body.

Julie wrote that she had asked Smith how the man could have just looked the other way while Russ Smith cremated his wife. Smith responded, "If I saved *your* son's life, wouldn't you be indebted to me?"

Julie had asked Smith how he knew what to do to cremate someone. Smith stated that Khris had been interested in the cremation process and they both had gone to see how it was done. Smith assured Julie he wasn't afraid that the man would talk. Smith also indicated to Julie that he had called his father and told him he had made a mistake, but Julie was uncertain if he had actually told his father the seriousness of the "mistake" he had made.

Julie's epistle turned from the dark side of Russ Smith's confession, although Julie claimed not to believe his words at the time, to the emotional side of their relationship.

Julie Moore had been divorced about two years and was ending an eighteen-month relationship when Russ Smith entered her life. She had no commitments and felt free to date whomever she chose. Following her second date with Smith, he told her he didn't want to see anyone else. He hoped she felt the same.

In her letter Julie painted a picture of bliss between herself and Smith. She had thought he was almost too perfect, but in retrospect she knew she had just wanted to see only the good in him. She admitted being scared, even though the relationship was so great, but as others had experienced, the perfect life with Russ Smith hadn't lasted.

Smith had wanted to sell his house on Thunderbay. When Julie asked where he would go, he'd said he thought he'd move in with her. Julie's first response had been to laugh. They hadn't been together long and, after all, she had a young son to consider. But in the end Russ Smith had gotten his way, as he was accustomed to doing, and had moved in.

Julie longed for her own home. In her letter to the task force, she rationalized that she couldn't afford a large place; that's when she and Smith began looking for a home to buy together. The house was much more than Julie could afford, but Smith had assured her he would help out. Actually, Smith had put all the money down on the house and put his name on the mortgage. Julie's name appeared only on the second title. She claimed Smith had said that if anything ever happened to him, she would always have a place to live.

Julie resided in the house with Smith only six months before moving with her son into a nearby town house. She stated she feared the judge would try to take her son from her because of her relationship with Smith. Julie wasn't going to let that happen. She didn't view her move as a breakup with Smith; they were merely living in separate residences. Smith evidently saw the living arrangements differently.

Julie wrote that Smith was gone most of the time, lying to her about his whereabouts. Smith told her he had met a woman named Mari in Grand Rapids. Not until a friend told her Smith had actually met Mari through Dateline personal ads, did she know the truth. Smith still had been coming round—making love to Julie—but when she learned the truth about his philandering, Julie broke off their relationship.

Apparently depressed over their breakup, Julie wrote that she had lost twenty-five pounds and had become ill. She finally deduced that her liaison with Smith was no longer worth the emotional pain. She wanted out of the relationship completely.

At that point Smith said he would stop seeing the other women and concentrate only on her. As long as she too would do whatever it took for them to stay together, Smith added. Within a week she discovered he had lied again. She gave him an ultimatum—it was either her or them. Smith chose to stay. Julie planned to move back into the house they had purchased.

According to her letter, Julie did move back into the house with Smith, but Smith moved out shortly after her return. He relocated in Monroe, Michigan. She was to follow him that summer. Smith hadn't mentioned marriage; it was to be just another convenient living arrangement between him and Julie, who had become little more than his "live-in girlfriend."

Bitterness laced Julie's letter as she described an incident regarding a car that Smith had purchased from a coworker at Firestone. Smith said he wanted Julie's name on the title and told her to pay the taxes on the vehicle. She did as Smith had asked.

Julie later came under investigation for sales tax fraud when a discrepancy was discovered between the amount of money the car was worth and the actual amount Smith had paid. Julie had been furious at Smith, telling him she was really scared and she wouldn't take the blame for something he did. Two days later, on Valentine's Day, Russ Smith proposed. Julie had expressed shock. Moore said yes, believing her married life with Smith would be as perfect as their dating life had been in the beginning. She was wrong.

"Things went <u>very sour from that moment!</u>" Julie wrote.

Julie moved to Monroe, Michigan, living in a house picked out by Smith. She didn't like her job. She didn't like the house. She and Smith weren't communicating, in or out of the bedroom. Their time together was spent either arguing or in silence. Finally Smith told Julie he wasn't in love with her and perhaps she should go back to Kalamazoo. She later learned Russ had already met Kara Scott, the latest in a long succession of women. The two had vacationed in Florida and planned to move there . . . all while Russ was still engaged to Julie.

On November 16, 1997, Julie had been involved in a car accident. Two days later, she and Smith finally broke up for good. She claimed they had remained friends, with Smith initially calling her once a week to check on her. She had even seen him a couple of times after the breakup. Things were actually better between them. He even apologized for the police talking to her, claiming he knew it had upset her.

Julie indicated that Smith had tried to keep in contact with Don Sewell and Bob Kilgore, his old friends at Sears, but both men had told him they didn't want anything else to do with him. Julie stated that both Don and Bob were angry that Smith had left his daughter in Ohio, when he could have chosen to stay near her.

Julie claimed that when Smith found out the CCC-CAT visited Ohio, he began rambling about the conversation he had had with Randy Dylhoff on his way to jail. He told her that was all the police had to go on and he couldn't even remember what he had said. After all, the conversation had occurred four years earlier.

Julie then recalled a time when she and Smith were talking about Khris one evening. He had said he didn't know where Khris was. Julie's letter drew a written picture of her looking at Smith oddly and telling him that that wasn't what he had told her. She reminded him of the story he had told her about how Khris had become angry, gotten a gun, and Smith had taken it away and shot her.

Russ responded with, "Oh yeah, I forgot I told you that story." He reminded her he had also told her he made the story up.

Perhaps unwisely, Julie had told Smith that she could make his life miserable because he'd admitted shooting Khris. But Smith had told her she couldn't make his life miserable, perhaps just make it a little uneasy for a little while. Julie had retorted that if anything ever happened to her, the first person they would look at was him.

"They'd have to prove it," Smith had replied.

When Sergeant Werkema read Judy's letter, a sly grin crossed his handsome face. He knew just how to use the letter to his advantage.

Chapter 24

On November 23, 1998, nearly eight weeks after talking with the Smiths in Lima, Werkema and Brown drove to the Auglaize Sheriff's Department, less than ten miles from Cridersville. There they met with John Bayliff of the Bayliff and Sons Funeral Home, based in Cridersville, Ohio. The white wood two-story building had been located just fifty feet across the alleyway from Roger and Linda Smith's home for more than thirty years. After reading Julie Moore's letter, detectives wondered if someone at the Bayliff and Sons facility had assisted Smith in disposing of his wife's body.

Mike Brown began the interview with John Bayliff by asking if Khristine Smith had ever made arrangements with him to be cremated. Bayliff confirmed that Khris, as well as Russ Smith, had come into the crematory expressing their desire to be cremated. In fact, at their request he had given both Russ and Khris a demonstration of how the crematory oven operated.

Werkema read the portion of the letter Julie Moore had written explaining how Russ Smith had disposed of his wife's body. He read the passage where Smith stated he had taken Khris's body in a barrel to Ohio, that a person at the funeral home was indebted to him for saving his daughter's life, and that he paid that person money to look the other way while he cremated Khris.

Bayliff stated he did have two daughters, but he was indebted to no one for saving either of their lives.

"Is your business monitored by an alarm?" Werkema asked.

Bayliff stated that his business wasn't alarmed and that if he were in his house, some fifty feet behind the crematory, watching the *Tonight Show,* which was his custom, he wouldn't be able to hear the gas meter if it were running at the crematory.

A key would have to be used to enter Bayliff's building, but John Bayliff told Werkema and Brown that the center bay door of the five-stall garage was not secured. For years anyone could merely jiggle the handle and the door would open, giving access to the garage area, which led directly to the crematory.

"John, in your opinion, did you have any employee capable of assisting Russ Smith with a cremation?" Brown asked.

After thinking for a minute, Bayliff stated that the first person to come to mind was John Garcia, a former employee who had left his employment under unfavorable circumstances.

Bayliff himself was fully cooperative, agreeing to take a polygraph test, to provide his business calendar, along with the files on both Khris and Russ Smith.

At that point Werkema and Brown left the Auglaize Sheriff's Department and followed Bayliff to his funeral home in nearby Cridersville. Pulling into the funeral home parking lot gave them an eerie feeling. The bright red and gold leaves of the surrounding trees were sharply contrasted by the lawn of deep green.

By four o'clock in the afternoon, Werkema and

Brown were reviewing Bayliff's files on the Smiths. Khris's file held a handwritten letter from her, inquiring about the cremation process. She stated that she and her husband were in the process of putting together wills and the subject of death had come up. Khris's letter was undated, but the copy of Bayliff's response to her was dated June 16, 1988, six years prior to her death, and shortly after Russ and Khris married.

The vital statistic portion of the form, indicating surviving relatives and authorization for cremation, had been completed by Russ Smith. He had signed the form. Under the service detail, nothing had been filled out. Russ Smith indicated that he wanted his remains scattered over a sunny hillside at the convenience or discretion of the funeral director.

Khris Smith had listed her surviving relatives as her father, Harry Klein Jr.; mother, Audrey (Kay) Klein; husband, Russell Smith; daughter, Lisa Smith; and brother, Troy William Klein. The authorization for cremation was signed by Khris Smith. She had indicated that she wanted her remains scattered over a lake or a sunny hillside, also at the convenience of the funeral director. On the back page of her file, on the memorandum, she had indicated she desired something plain and simple, nothing in the newspaper, no memory folders, no arrangements for family gatherings; any floristry was to be left with the funeral home or family members could take them, if desired. It was simply signed, Khristine Smith.

Werkema turned his head to look at Brown. Khris Smith wanted her ashes scattered on a lake. Perhaps Russ Smith hadn't dumped a barrel encasing her body after all, perhaps he had carried out his wife's last wish.

A third file, bearing the name of Lisa Smith, had

been completed in the handwriting of her mother. She too was to be cremated. However, Khris had left a provision so that when her daughter was old enough to make the decision, the final arrangements could be changed.

Khris indicated that if she, Lisa, and Russ were all killed in an accident, she wanted Lisa's ashes scattered with her own. And if Lisa was small enough, she wanted her to be cremated alongside herself.

A letter dated May 5, 1990, and addressed to Becky, one of John Bayliff's two daughters, was also in Lisa's file. Khris stressed that regardless of when either she or Lisa died, she wanted their ashes to be scattered in the same identical place.

The neighbors, friends, and relatives of Khris Smith had been right. There was a bond between the mother and daughter that seemed to be unbreakable. Khris Smith had even requested her daughter be with her in death. There was no way she would have ever left her child behind and merely vanished. Khris Smith was unquestionably dead.

John Bayliff obligingly gave the two Kalamazoo detectives a tour of the crematory area. The crematory machine itself was a large, rectangular-shaped box, blue in color and approximately six feet in height by twelve feet in length. The entire procedure was operated by eight buttons. The operator merely pushed a button to open the door, another to close the door; then the operator depressed a button to start the oven, and another to turn the oven off. Inside the blue box was the actual oven itself, made of brick. On top of the machine were three different-type rakes that were approximately eight feet in length with long metal handles. The rakes were used to scrape the remains out of the oven once cremation was completed. Bayliff explained that usually gloves were worn when the rakes were used because the oven continued to radiate heat while the raking of the ashes from the oven took place.

Werkema's eyes roamed the room. A brown Peg-Board laden with various tools, such as wrenches, pliers, screwdrivers, and tin snips, hung over a crude work-bench. Perhaps Smith had used one or more of the tools to cut the wedding ring from his wife's finger.

"Do you think there's a possibility we could get a latent fingerprint from the rakes?" Werkema asked. "Or one of Smith from the actual crematory room?"

Bayliff stated that it could be possible, but because he had shown the Smiths how the system worked, it might be likely a fingerprint was left at that time. He willingly agreed to let the Ohio Bureau of Criminal Identification and Investigation, as suggested by Werkema, process the crematory rakes for latent prints.

The following day the Ohio Bureau's Crime Scene Unit, located in Bowling Green, arrived in Cridersville. A glue-tank-type procedure, set up in the garage area of the funeral home, was used to raise the prints from the rakes. Latent prints were located, lifted, and tagged as evidence, then turned over to Detective Sergeant Mike Brown for chain of custody. John Bayliff allowed the detectives to keep as potential evidence the top portion of one rake where latent prints were located. The actual rake handle was hacksawed off, wrapped and secured in protective paper, and turned over to Brown.

At 1:20 P.M., on the day following the fingerprint collection, Brown and Werkema spoke with John Garcia, the former disgruntled employee of Bayliff and Sons Funeral Home. Garcia admitted he left Bayliff's employ in order to avoid being fired after working there

from 1987 until 1990. Garcia, speaking with a prominent Hispanic accent, described his duties as general
maintenance, such as snow removal and cleaning the
floors, along with performing cremations.

Werkema wanted Garcia to explain the cremation
process. Putting it plainly, Garcia stated that a body
would be brought into the cremation area already
prepped. He would put the body in a box, put it in the
oven, turn the oven on, and the oven would automati-
cally turn off after a couple of hours. Garcia would then
remove the remains, take them into the next room, and
smash the small portions of bone that were left into a
fine powder. He would then place the remains in a bag.
Werkema and Brown, accustomed to death in their jobs
as homicide investigators, listened dispassionately at the
matter-of-fact description of burning bodies.

Garcia admitted knowing Russ Smith and his
brother Rory as well as Khris, from their years in high
school. He claimed they weren't friends and didn't
travel in the same circles. At that point Garcia asked
why the officers were talking to him.

Werkema and Brown briefly explained, indicating
he was being questioned because he had been an employee of the Bayliff Funeral Home at the time Khris
Smith disappeared. They asked if he had helped dispose of Smith's wife's body.

Garcia's dark eyes widened. He adamantly denied
any involvement with Russ Smith or any assistance
with any cremation Smith may have had a part in.

He also denied helping Russ in remodeling the bathroom in Smith's Portage home. Garcia stated the
vehicle he drove at the time of Khris's disappearance
did not match the one seen at the Smith house around
that time.

As John Bayliff had done, Garcia readily agreed to undergo a polygraph examination to show that he was being truthful.

Detectives from the Cold Case Career Criminal Apprehension Team obtained permission to search from the new owners of the house that had once belonged to Khris and Russ Smith in Portage, Michigan. They were looking for evidence, perhaps undetected during a normal search, in the bathroom that had been determined to be where Khris Smith had been killed. The residents of the house were naturally reluctant to have a portion of their home dismantled, but they did cooperate with investigators.

The assigned search team took the bathroom apart even more meticulously than the Portage PD crime scene unit had done early in their investigation. The entire shower stall, including the porcelain tub, was removed. They hoped to find blood that may have possibly seeped into fine cracks and crevices between the tub and floor, although the likelihood seemed remote. Smith had scrubbed most of the bathroom thoroughly with bleach.

Satisfaction crossed the faces of members of the team as they saw a brownish stain beneath the tub fixture. Samples were taken and luminol was sprayed in the area in hopes it would show the substance to be positive for blood. The luminol spray was negative. However, lab tests on the samples taken would give them a definitive answer.

Just as Sergeant Mike Werkema had stated in his presentation to his fellow CCCCAT officers when presenting the Khris Smith case, he began to talk with members of Smith's family. He wanted them to hear the tape recording of Russ Smith confessing to murder. He wanted them all to know he was a killer.

Werkema saw the investigation as a domino game. One witness falls, they all talk. He also knew that witness participation was the biggest obstacle in any investigation, but he would work the plan and talk to everyone Smith knew.

Werkema traveled to the home of Rory Smith, Russ Smith's brother. Rory, who was baby-sitting with his children while his wife was out, agreed to meet the detectives at 4:00 P.M. at the Cridersville Police Department.

Rory was Russ's younger brother by three years. His father had told him about the detectives' visit and had told Rory to expect a call from them.

"What do you think of all this?" Werkema asked.

"I can tell you right now, I'm gonna sit right in this chair and tell you I have nothing to hide from you people," Rory said defensively. "I have absolutely no knowledge of anything to do with this."

Werkema thanked Rory for his candidness and shared the task force's mission of identifying the truth concerning Khris.

"Do you believe what we told your father? That Khris is, in fact, dead and that your brother is the person who caused her death?" Werkema asked.

"No, I don't believe it," Rory said flatly.

"There is a tape that has Russ's voice very clearly talking with Detective Dylhoff about the particulars. He was looking for a deal to work the situation out. I have that tape with me and I'm prepared to play it for you, if you would like to hear it. If you need that sort of evidence to believe what I'm telling you," Werkema stated.

He waited for Rory's response, hoping he, unlike his father, would be willing to hear the truth.

"I knew you'd ask me to hear the tape, but I don't want to hear it unless you make me," Rory said.

Werkema assured Rory he had no intentions of forcing him to listen to his brother's voice on the tape, that Khris was indeed dead, and that his brother Russ committed the murder.

Rory sat in silence, avoiding the eyes of the detective who watched him closely.

"We're very close to concluding our investigation and we're getting very close to traveling to Florida to speak with Russ. To give him an opportunity to speak with us," Werkema explained. "I don't want you to perceive me as some evil person or any member of my team. We are simply investigating police officers who are trying to do our job and seek out the truth."

"I understand that," Rory said. "I know you have a job to do. I'm very concerned about my father and his health."

Rory told the detectives that his father, Roger Smith, had a weak heart and had been under a great deal of stress. He feared that the investigation might cause his father to have a heart attack.

"I understand your concern," Werkema responded. "It's the nature of our job, and we, as police officers, need to do it. There is one person that can control all of this, who can stop all of this. That's your brother Russ. He is the one that is actually controlling what is going on and only he is capable of stopping it."

Rory paused momentarily before stating that he understood.

Werkema moved on to question Rory about the remodeling of the bathroom at Russ's house. Rory

denied helping remodel the bathroom. He acknowledged that he knew it had been done, but he insisted
he had not helped with the project. He also denied
driving to his brother's home a pickup truck like the
one identified by Russ's Portage neighbors. Likewise,
he denied any knowledge of Khris being cremated.

"That's why there will be no body," Werkema stated.
Remembering Dylhoff's field notes he added, "Our
investigation shows that a family member assisted
Russ in disposal of the body."

"So you're saying either I or my father or my brother
had something to do with this?" Rory asked with exas-
peration.

Werkema explained that he knew Roger Smith,
Rory, and Rick Smith, the other brother, loved Russ,
that it would be common sense to think they would
want to help him out, not knowing all the circumstances involved. Werkema's aim, he assured, was to
separate them from the independent actions of Russ.

"Last week we went back to Thunderbay and tore
the bathroom completely out, board by board, drywall by drywall. It has all been taken to the state
laboratory for microscopic examination. There is
some blood trace evidence that was found under the
bathtub, as well as some fingerprints located on the
back side of the shower enclosure and the drywall.
That will show us who assisted Russ in the repairs. It's
imperative that we identify that person. They were assisting in a cover-up," Werkema stated.

Werkema was lying. The brownish substance under
the tub hadn't proved to be blood and no fingerprints
had been recovered from the shower or drywall. It was
a bluff, a con to see how much Rory Smith knew
about the crime, and if he was involved. Werkema also

hoped Rory would pass the information on to Russ. He wanted Smith to sweat.

Rory reiterated that he hadn't been the one to help his brother make the repairs to his house and didn't know who did. He was more than willing to provide fingerprints for authorities and agreed to a polygraph.

"There's a strong case for murder and not manslaughter," Werkema stated. "And there's a strong indication that someone here in Cridersville assisted in disposing of the body. Your father is at the Auglaize Sheriff's Department being interviewed by the other half of our investigative team. He is being asked the same questions that I'm asking you."

"As I told you before, I had nothing to do with this. I know absolutely nothing," Rory said, his voice cracking as it filled with emotion and concern for his father.

"Do you think your father, out of love, helped Russ do this?" Werkema asked.

"No! No way," Rory insisted.

"How about your brother Richard?"

"No, he wouldn't either," Rory stated. "We are not that kind of people. We wouldn't do this."

Werkema was not so certain.

The detective again assured Rory that the task force knew with certainty that Russ had taken the life of his wife. "What do you think of your brother now?" Werkema asked.

"I don't know," Rory answered honestly. "We've been putting up with this shit for four years."

"Russ never told you anything about what this is all about?" Werkema asked.

"No."

As Chief John Drake of the Cridersville PD took Rory's fingerprints, Werkema watched in silence. He had hoped Rory would listen to his brother's taped confession, but his loyalty to Russ was strong. The Smith family was obviously a close-knit, caring family that found it impossible to believe that one of their members could commit cold-blooded murder. Werkema, on the other hand, had no problem believing Russ Smith was a killer.

The six-man investigative team kept busy interviewing anyone connected with Smith in Michigan and Ohio. They made numerous trips to Lima and Cridersville, talking with Smith's brothers and sister, and interviewing a number of men who had worked at the Bayliff and Sons Funeral Home.

On December 2, 1998, contact was made with Richard Smith, Russ's older brother. Rick, as he was known, was only 355 days older than Russ, but the brothers weren't close. Rick opted for public school, while Russ attended technical school. They didn't run in the same social circles and didn't share the same interests. In addition, Rick had moved away from home at nineteen, relocating to Detroit, Michigan.

Rick, like Rory, denied any involvement with the refurbishing of the upstairs bathroom on Thunderbay, the disappearance of his sister-in-law, or any unauthorized cremation that may have taken place at the Bayliff crematory.

"I really don't know anything," Rick Smith said, "and I really don't want to know anything. But Russ will have to pay the price and meet his Maker if he did do it."

The third, and final, sibling of Russ Smith was Wendy Smith Wertz. Russ's younger sister had first learned about the situation with her sister-in-law after returning from her honeymoon. She and her new husband had stopped by her parents' house upon their return.

Wendy, like Rory and Rick, wasn't close to Russ. He was six years her senior. He never confided in her; in fact, they seldom talked. Anything she knew about the case concerning Khris she had read in the newspaper.

Like her brothers, Wendy agreed to be polygraphed, if needed.

The cold-case squad had interviewed dozens of people. They told each one that Russ Smith was a killer. And just as detectives planned, the friends and family of Russ Smith began to call him at his residence in Navarre, Florida, ten miles from Fort Walton Beach in the Florida panhandle. Russ Smith knew for certain that a special task force was persistently digging into the disappearance of his wife. He knew that it was only a matter of time before they would be on his Navarre doorstep.

For three months Roger Smith had resisted offer after offer to listen to the recording of his son's conversation with Detective Dylhoff. Finally, during the first weeks of December 1998, he expressed a desire to hear for himself what was said between Russ and Dylhoff. He wanted no one else in his family to be there and asked that Werkema meet him at the Cridersville Police Department.

Werkema sat across from Roger Smith at a small table in one of the interview rooms. He depressed the play button on his recorder and watched the expressions of the elder man. Only subtle changes occurred in his expression during the conversation between the accused and the accuser, until Roger Smith heard a familiar sound made by his son.

"He's laughing at his family!" Roger Smith exclaimed

in amazement. "He has put my family through hell, and he's laughing at us."

Werkema could feel the pain that ripped at Roger Smith's heart. The entire Smith family had been loyal to Russ, standing up for him against everyone who thought him guilty of the unspeakable.

At the portion of the tape when Russ Smith began negotiating with the detective for manslaughter versus murder, Roger Smith said, "Stop! I've heard enough." He knew his son was guilty of murder.

Werkema's plan, however painful it was to the head of the Smith family, had worked. Roger Smith agreed to encourage his son to talk with the detectives.

There was one more cog to set in motion before Smith would be apprehended. Captain Dan Weston would use the news staff of the *Kalamazoo Gazette* to assist in the final calculated phase of the CCCCAT's plan to put pressure on Russ Smith to make a full confession.

Chapter 25

Headlines across the country announced the news of the impending impeachment hearings of President Bill Clinton for perjury, witness tampering, and abuse of power. But a headline on page C1 of the *Kalamazoo Gazette* caught the eye of many an interested reader, including the attorney representing Russ Smith. The headline read: POLICE FIND HOMICIDE EVIDENCE. A small photo of Russell Smith was included with the news copy.

The article boasted that a search of Russ Smith's former Portage residence yielded evidence that Smith had killed his wife, Khristine.

"It's true that we have searched the house and used a whole platoon of lab specialists to do it," Captain Dan Weston, head of the CCCCAT and member of the Kalamazoo Department of Public Safety, was quoted as saying.

Weston wouldn't specify what evidence officers located at the residence, but he believed Smith had shot his wife in a bathroom at the Portage house.

Werkema and Weston read the article with broad grins across their faces. They were certain that word of the news article would reach Smith soon. The bogus article had been placed in the paper to make Smith nervous, to make him feel the need to talk to someone—perhaps a family member or a friend who had spoken to investigators during their interviews, someone who would encourage him to talk to them. Werkema and Weston wished they could be there to see Smith's face when he read the article himself.

All six members of the CCCCAT drove to Navarre, Florida, in three separate vehicles. Their mission: to apprehend Russ Smith, return him to Kalamazoo, and have him indicted for murder.

The team ran a covert surveillance of Russ Smith and the house he shared with Kara Scott. Dan Weston and Mike Werkema were ready to follow Smith wherever he went. Other members of the cold-case squad would stay behind to execute a search warrant.

Smith drove to the nearby post office, where he retained a box for personal mail. Werkema and Weston watched from their car as Smith exited his vehicle and walked into the government building.

Weston and Werkema got out of the car and walked across the street. They found Russ Smith inside, reading a piece of mail.

"Hi, Russ, I'm Dan Weston," the captain said casually.

"I know," Smith stated, studying the piece of mail he had been reading. It was a copy of the *Kalamazoo Gazette* article planted by Weston. Smith's attorney had sent it.

"We want to talk to you, cop to cop," Werkema said. "We've talked to your daughter and to your dad. You need to call your father."

"You're right," Smith replied. "But let me go see Kara first."

It was an uncanny breakthrough. Some called it

luck, others consider it divine help. Whatever the odds of Smith reading the article he had planted in the paper, Weston believed it was unquestionably the beginning of Smith's psychological unraveling.

While Weston and Werkema were confronting Russ Smith at the Navarre post office, the remaining CC-CCAT officers were at Smith's residence. Mike Brown interviewed Kara Scott in the living room of her home while the other officers searched, room by room, looking for additional evidence against Smith.

When Brown explained to Kara that there was a warrant for Smith's arrest, the thirty-year-old girlfriend of the killer began to shout, "Where's the body? Where's the body?"

"Why would you ask that?" Brown inquired. "Has Smith talked with you about the murder?"

"No," Kara responded. "He told me the police believed he had something to do with Khris's disappearance, but I don't believe it. He has never admitted to me he did it."

Scott had known Smith for about a year and had been living with him for the past ten months. During their time together Smith had told her about having Lisa taken from him because he had moved her clothes into his bedroom. He had even told her Lisa had been examined for signs of child abuse but results were inconclusive.

When Smith told her he had a team of investigators looking into his ex-wife's disappearance, Kara had wanted to know what they would have on him *now* that they didn't have four years ago. Smith had said he didn't know.

"I asked him in a joking manner if he did it," Scott told Brown. "He said no."

As Kara Scott and Sergeant Brown talked, she continually glanced around the room nervously. She expressed concern about the officers who were searching her house and worried about the damage they might be causing.

"We have Russ in custody," Brown told her. "He is cooperating with the police and talking to them about the situation."

"I don't believe you," Kara retorted. "Russ couldn't hurt anyone."

Following his uneventful arrest, Russ Smith was booked into the Okaloosa County Jail. The phone call he'd been allowed to make to his father in Cridersville, Ohio, had prompted him to cooperate with authorities and waive extradition.

Mike Werkema and Dan Weston spent most of the night at the Okaloosa jail, interviewing Smith. He confessed to killing Khris but described a scene that didn't ring true to the veteran detectives.

Russ Smith admitted that he and Khris had fought the morning of September 28, 1994. He claimed she had spit in his face, causing him to overreact by pushing her forcibly against the glass shower door. Her weight had caused the glass to shatter, scattering hundreds of glass shards across the floor. Russ stated that as he was bent over to pick up the fragments of glass, Khris went to their bedroom, got a gun, and returned to the bathroom.

"My mistake was not leaving at that point," Smith confessed. "I grabbed the gun from her and shot her."

He claimed to have discarded her body, still encased in the black barrel, in Lake Erie.

On December 16, 1998—four years, two months, and eighteen days after Khristine Smith was mur-

dered—Russ Smith and members of the CCCCAT
began the two-day journey from Navarre, Florida, to
Kalamazoo, Michigan. Two additional cars, with two
CCCCAT members each, traveled with them, taking
turns driving their prized prisoner back to justice.

Before leaving the Okaloosa County Jail, Mike
Brown read Russ Smith his Miranda rights. Smith assured Brown he knew his rights, reminding him he
was once a police officer himself. It was going to be a
long trip. On the chance that Russ Smith decided to
talk with his escorts about the events of September 28,
1994, they wanted to make sure all legal loopholes
were closed. They didn't want another confession that
wouldn't stand up in court.

Mike Werkema and Mike Brown took the first shift
of escorting their prisoner. Werkema drove the
Chevrolet Monte Carlo, with Weston riding "shotgun," and Smith handcuffed and in leg irons in the
backseat. They drove a two-door police department
vehicle, selected for its security of no back doors and
its lack of markings for anonymity.

Smith sat back and watched as the palm trees of
northern Florida filed by.

Shortly after the trio of cars was under way, Smith
asked if anyone had talked to his folks, Lisa, or Kara
since the previous night. Werkema offered to let
Smith use his cellular phone to call and let his family
know he was on his way to Michigan.

"The cheering-up committee," Smith remarked, referring to Werkema's offer. "He's got a good heart."

Smith held the phone to his ear with some difficulty. It was Kara he chose to call. When she answered,
Smith said, "I'm okay. Three sets of handcuffs, but
they put them on very comfortably. It's going to be a

long car ride, I'm sure. I'm kind of stiff-necked. I didn't sleep very well, but I got a chance to get a shower this morning and all that good stuff."

Smith seemed surprisingly upbeat for a man who had just spent the first of what would be many nights in jail.

"How's Katelyn?" Smith asked, referring to Kara's daughter.

"Know that I love you. I wish things hadn't turned out this way," Smith said. "Everything okay with my mom and dad? Lisa okay? She wouldn't talk to me last night. I'm sure the reality is going to hit her very soon. I wish I could be there with her, but all I can do is be there *for* her."

There was a pause, indicating that Kara was speaking on the other end. Then Smith said, "I love you too. You doing okay? Try to pull yourself together because I know you have to work today. Know that I love you very much. I'll try to call you tonight, okay? I love you too. Try to have a good day. Be strong. I love you too. Bye."

As Smith awkwardly handed the phone to Dan Weston, he said, "Thank you very much."

Smith asked Werkema how far they planned to drive that day, with Werkema replying that it would be about eight hours.

"Do you mind if I call her again tonight?" Smith asked.

"No, but what we have to do is get to a facility tonight. When we stop, we'll make sure you get your phone calls," Werkema replied.

The team had made arrangements to stop over in Franklin, Tennessee, where Smith would be lodged overnight in the Williamson County Jail. Under law a prisoner could not be transported more than ten hours a day. They would pick him up the following morning, again read him his Miranda rights, and complete the trip to Kalamazoo.

Smith sat back, resting his head against the seat.

"It sure is pretty down here," Werkema remarked.

"Yeah. Did you get a chance to go to the beach?" Smith asked, as if Werkema and Weston were on a vacation.

"No. We did go to a great Irish pub last night."

"McQuire's?" Smith asked.

"Yes."

McQuire's was a well-known bar in the area that boasted approximately $70,000 was pasted on their ceiling. The McGuire's in Pensacola claimed nearly $200,000.

"I understand there's a lot of aids down here in Florida," Werkema remarked.

"The AIDS virus?" Smith asked.

"Rolaids, Band-Aids, hearing aids," Werkema said with a laugh. "That's the only Florida joke I know."

Werkema was putting Smith at ease, utilizing the humorous buddy method. If Smith relaxed and let down his guard, he might tell them everything they wanted to know about how he murdered Khris and where her body could be found.

"When I talked to your dad, your whole family, I said, people make mistakes. Anybody that says they haven't made a mistake is lying. When people make a serious mistake like this, they panic. Once you realize you made the mistake and the law has come down on you, you have to be up front about the whole thing," Weston stated.

"This is the right thing to do," Werkema added.

"I know it is," Smith replied. "I really know it is. I should have done this a long time ago."

Smith watched the scenery for a while, then asked, "How long do you think this is going to take in court?"

"Well, I know one thing," Werkema said, "the investigation is far from over. Everything has to be told. We can't go with half the story, it has to be complete, and it has to be totally true."

During their conversation Werkema and Weston discussed the people they had interviewed during the investigation, accounting for more than two thousand man-hours. Werkema explained that they had been attempting to find the person or persons who had helped Smith cover up the death of his wife. Smith insisted there was no one else, but the detectives doubted his words.

Unable to see the tape recorder sitting on the front seat between the two detectives, Smith was unaware every word was being recorded.

"The system works when all the facts are known and all the truth is out," Werkema stated. "The story you told us last night, was it the whole truth?"

"Yes."

"Why did you tell Julie Moore a different story?"

"I wanted to get her off my back. She kept nagging at me," Smith said.

"Do you remember telling her you had someone else help you get rid of the body?" Werkema prodded.

"It was a bullshit story," Smith retorted.

"Do you remember taking money from your bank before you left for Ohio?"

"I guess so. I wouldn't have gone out of town without money," Smith answered.

"Can you see why we would think there was someone else? Someone you paid to help you?" Werkema questioned.

"Yes."

"Did you have a demonstration of how the crematory worked?" Werkema asked.

"Yeah," Smith said with a little laugh. "Oddly enough, it was Khristine's idea to do that," Smith added.

"Russ, did you cremate Khris?" Werkema asked bluntly.

"No. Absolutely not," Russ answered.

"Who helped you fix the bathroom?" Brown asked.

"Nobody. There was only one person who helped me fix a water leak. That was it," Smith said, his voice beginning to sound tired.

"How did you get the bathtub enclosure out?" Werkema wanted to know.

"Pieces. Do you know what aviation snippers are? They're angled cutting tools to cut metal. I used them to cut up the enclosure," Smith explained.

"Where did you take the pieces?" Werkema asked.

"A Dumpster in the subdivision for new homes."

"How did you fit Khris's body in the barrel?" Brown inquired.

"It wasn't a problem. Picked her up and put her in," Smith said almost lightheartedly.

Smith confirmed that the barrel he used to put his wife's body in was from Sears. He had used an everyday-type ax to punch holes in the barrel on the sides, along the bottom, after tying the barrel to the boat with rope. As it floated in the water, he had struck it with the ax repeatedly to insure it would sink.

Smith stated he had driven around with Khris's body in the back of his truck, encased in the barrel, for four days before borrowing a boat to dispose of the body.

"What you're telling us sounds very illogical," Werkema said.

"Why's that?" Smith asked.

"It doesn't make sense that you would drive around with her body in a barrel in the back of your truck for four days when you could have been stopped and the body discovered. It doesn't make sense that you drove immediately to Ohio but left the body in your truck. With all the lakes in your area, it doesn't make sense to go all the way to Lake Erie to dispose of the body. And from the time you dropped Lisa off to the time you made that first phone call, there is at least six hours of your time not accounted for," Werkema explained.

Werkema felt certain that during the six-hour time lapse, Smith hadn't been driving to Florida, as he had stated. He believed Smith had been inside the crematory, seventy-five yards from his parents' home, where his daughter slept, disposing of her mother's body. He recalled the Peg-Board he had seen inside the Bayliff and Sons facility and wondered if Smith had used one of the tools hanging there to cut Khris's wedding ring from her hand. It would have been difficult, at best, for Khris to cut it off herself, as Smith had insisted.

"Do you recall when you were talking to Randy, saying you didn't want anybody else charged with this?" Brown questioned. "That tells us right away someone else helped."

"I told him that so he'd go looking somewhere else and stay away from me," Smith replied.

"Those are the things we have to get answered," Werkema said. "It doesn't matter if you took her body to Lake Michigan, if you took Khris down to the gravel pits, or you cremated her, or buried her, that isn't relevant to what's going on. That's not going to change the outcome of this."

"Absolutely no one helped me. I'm not protecting anyone," Smith said emphatically. "I busted my ass putting that house back together."

"What about the six hours between when you dropped Lisa off at your parents' and when you made the first call?" Werkema asked.

Smith insisted he had driven down Highway 75, gotten off at one point, and had driven around looking for a place to dump Khris's body.

Smith sighed heavily. He appeared aggravated by the constant barrage of questions.

"Where did you shoot Khris?" Werkema asked. "What part of her body?"

Again Smith heaved an audible sigh. "Can we not talk about this right now?" he asked. He had had enough of their questions. They had only been in the car for a couple of hours; he dreaded the prospect of two days of continuous interrogation.

At lunchtime Werkema pulled into a restaurant not far from the highway. Smith, still in handcuffs, was escorted inside and positioned beside Dan Weston and across from Werkema.

When the waitress asked for their orders, Smith, scruffy from not shaving, his graying reddish hair tousled, smiled his most charming smile and asked for a hacksaw as he displayed his bound hands.

He seemed to enjoy his burger and fries as Weston and Werkema played the roles of friend and confidant. Weston even rubbed Smith's back as he attempted to have his prisoner relax and feel unthreatened.

It was more than Werkema could take. He kicked
Weston under the table while he worked hard to sup-
press a laugh.

Back on the highway, Werkema again drilled Smith
about the events of the day his wife died. He took on
the approach of "cop to cop," working on Smith's ego
and pride that he was a former police officer. Then,
in order to get Smith to identify with him, he began
dissing Khris.

"I know Khris was a slut. We know you shot the
bitch," Werkema stated, not believing one derogatory
word he was saying about Khristine Smith. "Where did
you shoot her? What part of her body?" Werkema
asked again.

"In the temple," Smith confessed.

Smith's earlier account of how the murder happened hadn't made sense. If they had struggled over
the gun, more than likely Khris wouldn't have been
shot in the temple. Smith was still lying.

"Russ, you got what you wanted all along. You won.
Lisa is with your folks, just like you wanted. She is well
taken care of. You need to go ahead and tell us the
truth," Werkema encouraged.

There was a long silence before Werkema spoke
again.

"For Khris to have been shot in the temple, she
would have had to be on her knees," he surmised.

Tears filled the tired eyes of Russ Smith. For four
years he had hidden the truth about how Khris had
died. For four years he had lived with the lies, deceit,
and guilt of her murder. It was time to tell the truth.

"Khris and I did argue that morning. She threatened
to leave. While she was in the shower, I went to the bedroom and got a .380 chrome-plated handgun. She was

bent over, washing her face. I raised the gun and shot her in the left temple. A second shot was waist high and went into the shower wall. That's why I had to replace the whole shower and tub," Smith confessed, crying as he spoke.

Finally Russell Smith was admitting he'd gone to the bedroom to get the gun. There had been no struggle. Russ Smith had cold-bloodedly killed his wife.

Chapter 26

As Russell Smith was on his way back to Kalamazoo County to face indictment for the murder of his wife, Khristine, her mother was remembering her only daughter's birth thirty-two years earlier. Kay Klein wouldn't be celebrating Khris's birth, instead she was mourning her death. The only comfort Kay could take in Khris's absence was the joy she felt knowing her daughter's killer was finally being brought to justice.

For four years Russ Smith had been enjoying his freedom. He had acquired a new job, a new house, a new woman, and a new stepdaughter to take the place of all the things he had lost from his one selfish act of murderous rage. Now, with the balmy Florida breezes behind him, Smith's hopes for his future were as cold as the frigid Michigan air.

Russ Smith's confession to the murder of his wife gave Dan Weston and his dedicated team of detectives only partial satisfaction. To Weston and his men, the job was unfinished.

There were glaring flaws in Smith's account of the disposal of his wife's body. The six-hour gap in time— from when Smith arrived in Cridersville, Ohio, and when his telephone records indicated he first called home allegedly to see if Khris had returned—had not satisfactorily been accounted for. The question in

Weston's mind and the minds of his officers remained: where was Khris Smith's body?

Smith's arraignment before Judge Robert Kropf gave the cold-case squad no new leads in their quest to find Khris's body.

When Judge Kropf asked Smith if he understood the charge of open murder that had just been read to him, Smith simply replied, "Yes, sir, I do."

Dressed in a green golf shirt and blue jeans, his hands handcuffed in front of him, Smith had nothing further to say to the court.

Assistant prosecutor Stuart Fenton, his red hair closely cropped and his wire-rimmed glasses perched atop his prominent nose, addressed the court. The meticulously attired young prosecutor asked Kropf to deny bond, citing Smith's contacts in Ohio and Florida and stating that Smith had "the motive to run."

Smith sat dispassionately as his attorney, James Hills, fought the no-bond request. Hills pointed out that Smith hadn't been hiding in the three years he had been gone from the Portage, Michigan, area; he had been living openly in his new home in Florida, working, and maintaining a residence.

"He voluntarily returned to Michigan to face the charge," Hills stated, hoping Smith's willingness to face the court would work in his favor. Kropf, however, wasn't impressed.

"These are the most serious charges we have in Michigan," Kropf announced as he denied the bond request. Russ Smith would remain in custody.

The CCCCAT had collected evidence in both Smith's house on Thunderbay in Portage, as well as additional evidence in Navarre, Florida. With Smith securely in jail, their investigation would continue. Captain Weston and his men still believed that Smith hadn't acted alone in disposing of Khris's body. From neighbors in Smith's Portage community, who had described a red pickup parked beside Smith's house and seeing a man about Smith's height who was similar in looks to Smith, the team of detectives had a strong idea of who the accomplice might be. They intended to probe further into their unnamed suspect's involvement, but their highest priority remained finding Khris Smith.

Dr. Robert Sundick was the head of the anthropology department at Western Michigan University in Kalamazoo. Dan Weston was pleased to have such a well-respected anthropologist in their midst. He was just the person to aid in the search for Khris Smith's body.

"Dr. Dirt," as Dr. Sundick was dubbed by the cold-case squad, arrived at the former Smith home on Thunderbay with a truckload of excavating equipment and a dozen of his best students.

The new owners of the house shuddered. They had done their best to cooperate with police—to be good citizens. First they had given permission for the upstairs bathroom to be dismantled piece by piece, causing a cloud of dust to settle on everything in the house, not to mention a total renovation project to tackle. Now their green grass was being staked and burrowed. They wondered if it would ever be over.

The Smiths' former property was enclosed on two sides by a four-foot chain-link fence. The back of the lot was closed off by a neighbor's eight-foot wooden fence adorned at the top with a two-foot lattice strip.

Dr. Sundick and his team began by mapping out a grid, then driving foot-tall yellow stakes into the ground to serve as markers. A square wooden box with wire mesh in the bottom was suspended by a chain on a tall wooden tripod. The screened box would be used as a sieve for sifting the dirt. Blue tarps were spread over the ground next to areas designated for digging. Dr. Sundick, dressed in khaki pants and a heavy blue jacket, wore a bright red ball cap to protect his head and thinning white hair from the cold.

WMU students used shovels to dig a six-foot square patch of ground, carefully removing the grass and some six inches of earth beneath it. The dirt would be sifted for any evidence pertaining to the Khris Smith murder. But after hours of intensive work, no evidence of Khris Smith could be found in her former backyard.

Russ Smith continued to insist he had dumped his wife's body in Lake Erie. Smith told of transporting his wife's corpse in a steel drum with a metal band around the top, secured by a single nut and a bolt. He claimed he had put the drum in the back of his 1990 Dodge Dakota pickup and towed a sixteen-foot gray-and-white boat behind him. Smith stated he drove to Toledo, Ohio, and then specifically to Cullen Park. Smith stated he dumped his wife's body, along with the murder weapon, in Maumee Bay, east of Toledo, Ohio.

"I launched the boat at Cullen Park," Smith told Detective Sergeant Mike Brown. "There's an island approximately seven miles out from Cullen Park. I dumped the gun and the barrel with Khris's body, somewhere halfway between the Cullen Park boat launch and the island."

Smith indicated his story could be corroborated by a Toledo police officer who, Smith claimed, had seen him at the boat launch and had asked what he was doing. According to Smith, he told the officer he was going night fishing. Even though Smith's story couldn't be confirmed by the Toledo PD, the cold-case detectives decided to send out a search-and-rescue vessel in an effort to locate the barrel. They knew it was a long shot, but their determination to find Khris Smith's body drove them to take whatever measures available to them in their efforts to bring her home.

A coast guard cutter, fully equipped with sonar equipment, was called into action. They patrolled the area designated by Smith, making a grid of the multimile radius. Nothing the size of a fifty-five-gallon barrel was detected by the coast guard vessel.

They decided to take Smith out for a boat ride. If he could pinpoint the exact location of where he dropped the barrel, they would be prepared for a dive team to go in after it.

A large boat, complete with sonar equipment, was chartered by the CCCCAT to take Russ Smith, Detective Richard "Butch" Mattison, and a dive team provided by the Detroit Police Department to the vicinity where Smith claimed he had dropped the body.

Dressed in bright red insulated suits, complete with black rubber gloves and snug hoods to protect them from the frigid cold, Smith, Mattison, and the dive team officers set out to find the deepwater grave where Smith contended he'd dropped his wife's body.

On their first pass they located a large sail mast resting on the lake bottom, but nothing the size of a fifty-five-gallon barrel showed up on their sonar screen. On their second pass the mast was again spotted, but as before, no barrel was detected.

Finding a sail mast, not once but twice, and failing

to locate anything the size of the barrel, reinforced
the team's gut feeling that Khris Smith's body hadn't
been disposed of in the manner Russ Smith claimed.

Search efforts were hampered by twelve-foot swells
that broke over the bow of the boat and kept the men
on deck scrambling to maintain their footing. The
dark clouds overhead threatened to blow in even
more rough weather. The tall, stout figure of Mattison
swayed as the lake spray pelted his face, occasionally
obscuring his vision. Smith, standing beside him, appeared to have lost his sense of direction, unable to
give a precise location of the barrel he claimed to
have thrown into the deep waters of the lake. White-
caps blanketed the water's surface. Mattison was
forced to call off the search.

When the detectives and Smith arrived at the dock
in the small rubber craft used to navigate close to
shore, the police radio attached to Mattison's belt
slipped loose, falling unnoticed into the murky waters
below. When Mattison was unable to account for the
police-issue radio, Sergeant Werkema wrote on the
equipment manifest, "Radio lost at sea." He had no
idea his entry had been true.

Smith had had enough—the years of looking behind
him, waiting for the police to show up; the distance he
had created between him and Lisa; the pain he had
caused his parents; the lies, the deceit. He wanted it all
to end.

Russ Smith agreed to plead guilty to second-degree
murder in the death of his twenty-eight-year-old wife.
He didn't want to go through a lengthy, complicated
trial, or through the scrutiny of his turbulent mar-

riage and his decision to end it, permanently. Second-degree murder was a good deal for Smith. A court trial could net him murder in the first, which could result in life in prison. He couldn't take that chance.

Standing before Kalamazoo County circuit judge William Schma, listening to preliminary queries, Russell Smith remained mute. Finally Judge Schma asked the key question, "Tell me what you did that makes you believe you are guilty of the crime of second-degree murder?"

Smith, dressed in a dark suit, white shirt, and tie, paused a few long moments while the courtroom became eerily quiet. Finally Smith broke a four-year public silence about the day his wife, Khristine Smith, was murdered.

Smith swallowed hard before speaking. "After a verbal, and slight physical, altercation with my wife, I went and got a gun and shot her." Smith admitted his wife died on September 28, 1994, and that he had intended to kill her.

Judge Schma set the final plea hearing for March 8, 1999, when he would formally sentence thirty-six-year-old Smith to prison. Although not bound by law to accept the agreement made between the prosecution and the defense of thirty-five to seventy years, the judge could choose to give Smith life, but judges tend to honor plea agreements. If Schma followed the usual path, Smith wouldn't be eligible for parole for thirty-five years. Michigan gave no good time for serving sentences for violent crimes, therefore Smith would have to serve the minimum of thirty-five years.

On the day of Russ Smith's final sentencing, the Kalamazoo County courtroom was filled to capacity. Behind a row of newspaper reporters and television cameramen huddled the tiny figure of Lisa Smith, nestled between Linda and Roger Smith. The grandparents' arms hugged Lisa protectively as all eyes were on the girl who wore bibbed denim overalls with a smiling figure of Tigger, Winnie the Pooh's pal, embroidered on the front. Lisa appeared vulnerable and younger than her eleven years.

It was the day before Lisa's twelfth birthday. Another birthday she'd celebrate without her father or mother.

Stuart Fenton, assistant prosecutor, stood at the front of the courtroom. Attired in a well-tailored suit, Fenton was the image of conservative Kalamazoo politics except for the small gold stud in his left earlobe. He waited with the court gallery for Russell Smith to enter the courtroom.

Sitting at the front of the courtroom, Judge Schma was positioned in front of the great seal of the state of Michigan, flanked by the American flag on his right and the state of Michigan flag on his left. He watched along with spectators as Russ Smith entered the courtroom, escorted by two bailiffs. The room fell silent. Only the clanking shackles on Russ Smith's ankles could be heard until the whimpering sobs of his tearful daughter filled the air.

Smith's hair had lost most of its reddish brown hue. In his three-year absence from Kalamazoo County, he had turned mostly gray. His expression was solemn. His eyes avoided the crowd.

When Smith glanced behind him to his family, his guise was one of distress but void of regret. He watched his daughter's tears roll down her cheeks.

Lisa Smith's tears persisted throughout the prosecutor's statements. She learned how her father had deliberately and with malice taken the life of her mother. Her tears continued as her maternal grandfather addressed the court, telling the judge that on the day his daughter was reported missing, he knew she was dead.

"He's been laughing at everybody, laughing at all of us and getting away with it," Harry Klein Jr. said of his former son-in-law. Klein's words were filled with anger and bitterness. He hadn't been close to Khris in her last years, but he had loved her nonetheless.

Lisa Smith began to sob louder as her father rose to address the court. Her tears fell for her lost mother and for the lies concerning her disappearance. She whimpered, grieving for time lost with her mother.

But Lisa Smith's flood of emotions really erupted when her father was sentenced to thirty-five to seventy years in prison for firing two bullets from a handgun into Khristine Klein Smith's head while she showered in their Portage home.

Smith's accomplice, if indeed there had been one, was never found, but Russell Smith had finally been brought to justice for his crime. Not a crime of passion but one of calculated premeditation. Khristine Smith's murderer was finally sentenced to prison for her death.

The Cold Case Career Criminal Apprehension Team had taken only five months to secure an arrest and conviction. They were proud of their efforts but saddened that a young girl would spend her life without a mother. They couldn't bring Khris Smith back from death, but they were pleased to have brought some closure for her family and Russ Smith to justice.

Epilogue

Randy Dylhoff remains a detective with the Portage Police Department.

Russ Smith is serving his sentence in the Carson City, Michigan, facility of the Michigan prison system. Smith refused a requested interview, stating he would rather tell Lisa the truth about her mother himself.

Smith, who must serve a minimum of thirty-five years, will more than likely serve more. No inmate in Michigan has ever been granted parole on their first attempt.

Lisa Smith continues to reside with her adoptive parents (Linda and Roger Smith) in Cridersville, Ohio. She is maturing into a vibrant young woman.

The success rate of the CCCCAT has been phenomenal. The five-member team, plus Captain Dan Weston, solved eight of the eight cases assigned to them. In baseball terms they batted a thousand.

Members of the team rotate off the squad every two years and only one original member, **Richard Mattison,** remains, along with **Dan Weston** of the Kalamazoo Department of Public Safety, who continues to oversee the CCCCAT. Of the team who solved the Khris Smith case, **Mike Brown** has retired from law enforcement; **Mike Werkema** was promoted to lieutenant with the Kalamazoo Police Department and is now a shift commander in the uniformed division; **Ron Petroski** is back with the Portage Police Department; **Greg Hatter** is with the Kalamazoo PD in the major-case homicide unit.

The Kalamazoo cold-case squad is respected and duplicated throughout the country. Mike Werkema has traveled to Tennessee, Alabama, and Illinois, teaching the team's concept and organizational structure to others in the field of law enforcement.

"One of the greatest satisfactions for a cold-case detective is helping family members put closure on a murder case. It is such a pleasure when you see the gleam in their eyes," Werkema says. "It's like a ton of bricks has been taken off them."

A new team of cold-case officers, which includes two women, is now tackling unsolved crimes in Kalamazoo County, with equal success.

Here are some other cold cases undertaken by the original CCCCAT—these killers, like Smith, thought they had gotten away with murder.

Brothers Arraigned in 1982 Killing

In 1982 four masked men strolled into the Corkscrew Party Store in Kalamazoo, Michigan, went to the office in the rear of the store, then shot and killed Michael Linstrom, a store employee, as he attempted to wrestle with the intruders. Sixteen years later, a trio of brothers—Jerry, Roy, and Terry Traylor—and a friend were apprehended by the cold-case homicide team headed by Captain Dan Weston.

"We were able to locate people that knew information they were withholding in 1982 and 1983 when it was originally investigated," Captain Weston said. "There is a point where these cases should be relooked at because people's loyalties change. Witnesses and people the perpetrators may have confided in—relatives, friends, girlfriends—may have been afraid of the perpetrators and afraid to be honest and come forward with information to the authorities."

Patrick and Robert Gray Charged in 1988 Killings

A Cadillac pulled up to Austin Lee Garrett as he lay in the road from a gunshot wound. Two men emerged and stood over Garrett, shooting him again before climbing into their car and roaring off down the street. The case, unsolved for more than a decade, was taken on by the cold-case team. They located Timothy Sanders, who had been using drugs with Garrett and had witnessed brothers Robert and Timothy Gray shoot the victim.

Due to the investigative efforts of the cold-case homicide team, the Gray brothers were convicted of murder.

Woman Identifies Killer Twenty Years Later

A woman who was only eleven-years-old at the time Cornell Smith was viciously beaten with a baseball bat, had snuck out of her house and witnessed the brutal crime. Not until almost two decades later, when contacted by the cold-case homicide team, did Gail Johnson know Smith had died from the blows. She remembered the incident well and even led detectives to the place where Smith's attacker had stashed the bat. With the face of the man she saw swing a bat at Smith emblazoned on her memory, she picked out the killer from a photo lineup.

Dan Weston's team of investigators located Johnson from a photograph that had been taken the day of the killing. She had been standing on the street wearing

jeans and a pink shirt. Once Johnson had been identified and contacted by the CCCCAT, she positively
identified Martin Lewis as Smith's killer. The team
learned Johnson, who was eleven years old at the time
of the killing, hadn't come forward then because she
feared punishment for being out of the house without
permission.

1995 Murder Case Reopened

Randee Ashby was the bright light of her family.
Two days before being inducted into the Comstock
National Honor Society, the cute, active fourteen-year-
old was raped and murdered while baby-sitting for
her sister's children. Before leaving the murder scene,
the attacker used a child's garment and a blanket
from the basement to clean himself. These items provided vital information to the CCCCAT.

Arrest Made in 1990 Slayings

In 2001, through the efforts of the cold case squad,
Jeff Titus, former police officer, U.S. Marine, and
firearms instructor for the Michigan National Guard
was arrested for killing two hunters in the Fulton State
Game Area eleven years earlier. Both men, wearing
orange hunting gear, had been shot in the back.

CCCCAT officers discovered Titus's alibi given
years earlier didn't hold up. He was convicted of the
murder.